PRAISE FOR CYBER RANTS

"In Cyber Rants, Fuller and Silent Sector combine their deep understanding of the complexities of Cybersecurity, a refreshing sense of humor and an appropriate dose of irreverent ranting to create a book you'll want to read, make notes in, and keep within reach. If you're a business leader, this belongs on your must-read list."

—Stephen Neff,
CEO, Neff Healthcare

"Cyber Rants and the team at Silent Sector provide a principled approach to proactive cybersecurity. Cyber Rants balances plain talk with technical detail to drive the message home."

—Steve Bradley,
Cybersecurity Leader, IBM

"As Cyber Rants reveals, cybersecurity has to emphasize mindset, experience, and simple processes which in turn may help build a culture assisted by technology. Organizations fail as a result of taking a tools/technology first approach."

Michael Guggemos,
COO & CIO from Emerging Ventures to Global Fortune 500s

"Every day we hear about another business being the victim of cyber-attack. Is there an affordable and effective way for company leaders to protect their business, their staff and their customers? *Cyber Rants* answers those questions in an entertaining, informative and useful way. And this very readable and entertaining guide provides special emphasis on the most deep and painful type of cyber wounds.... the self-inflicted!"

—Scott Celley,
Managing Partner, Trifecta Communications

"Cybersecurity isn't optional in today's world. With a little humor and a lot of information, *Cyber Rants* breaks down the marketing hype and what sales teams often fail to explain. *Cyber Rants* can help save business leaders time and money, and will definitely alleviate a lot of headaches as you learn what makes a difference in protecting your company."

—Heather Monthie, PhD,
Associate Dean of Technology, Grand Canyon University,
Author and Podcast Host, HeatherMonthie.com

"As the security professional is from an eclectic group of individuals; from coders, hackers, attorneys, musicians, biologists, psychologists, business people and of course the techie, this book reflects the views and opinions about the challenges that we all face in securing a virtually total unsecure-able but critical business asset."

—Rich Owen,
Chief Evangelist, Johnny Security Seed LLC
Creator Infosec program for Mission Operations,
Johnson Space Center, NASA

"The information that these three Experts have been able to combine into one book is absolutely unreal; and I would expect nothing less from Michael Rotondo, Lauro Chavez, and Zach Fuller. These are without a doubt, the "Experts" of the cyber security industry in my opinion. Zach and Team, thanks for combining your skillsets to create a book that is great for early tech Founders like myself; it helped me to learn cyber security in a hurry."

—Ty Smith,
Founder, CEO of Vigilance Risk Solutions

"Cybersecurity isn't optional in today's world and *Cyber Rants* tells you what the industry's sales and marketing hype fails to explain. A little humor and ranting with a lot of information, this book will save you time, money, and a lot of headaches as you learn what makes a difference in protecting your company."

—Jason Veiock,
Head of Corporate Security for a Global Technology Company

"*Cyber Rants* strikes a balance between informal real-speak talk, being direct and honest, and that of consultation experienced outcomes and rants. Rants, in this book, are actually the truths we all scream as consultants for our stakeholders and clients to align towards, adopt, and champion towards maturing their cyber security risk management outcomes."

—Ken Dunham,
Global Distinguished Fellow & Cybersecurity Thought Leader

"I have been in Information Technology for almost 50 years, I have seen the fads come & have seen the fads go. Cyber Security is not a fad, many of my clients in almost every industry have been hacked, the CFO of a large hospital told me, "when you get hacked it is not only the money involved, or the damage to your reputation but the 17 Class action law suits that takes executive focus and time away from the business." Cyber Security is not an Information Technology issue but a Corporate issue, it should be ingrained in the culture of the Corporation, it should be how they do business. Cyber Security looks like a daunting task, but this book will help to give insights & thoughts how to start & move forward, I know the guys involved have worked with them & they are real Security Pros. Keep in mind the old proverb: The longest journey stars with the first step."

—John Nickerson,
Principal, COZA Technologies

"This book makes clear the cyber security risks businesses face, and what to do about them, in terms that even non-technical leaders can understand and appreciate. The authors' wit, insight and candor make Cyber Rants an enjoyable read, as well as a valuable investment of time."

—Nancy Stone,
Principal, Stone Strategic Management

"An excellent primer to secure technology in an era of advanced persistent threats and complete reliance on technology."

—Paulo Shakarian, Ph.D.
CEO and Co-Founder, CYR3CON

"I loved this Book! Most people believe that cybersecurity is a problem that revolves around security tools, software and programs; the authors clearly state that; 'the human element is both the primary problem and the solution in the fight against cybercrime.'

While it might feel challenging to keep up with the demand for Technical Talent, there are other, mostly overlooked, issues contributing to many cybersecurity struggles. This book highlights the complexity and costs involved in finding the right expertise and guidance to keep up with the changing compliance requirements, evolving threats, and workforce challenges.

Over the last 25 years, I have conducted more than 20,000 interviews, head-hunted, placed and coached dozens of Senior Executives; IT Professionals & Senior Security Specialists up-level their Careers. After witnessing 'superstars' working tirelessly to stay ahead of threats to protect their organizations and our economy, I know that Cybersecurity Experts are a different 'breed!' Cyber Rants will help you better understand them, know who you need on your team, what to watch out for and, most importantly, how to retain them.

This book will give you a 'behind the curtain' inside view of so much that you need to know, and save you tons of regret, if you implement and take the guidance seriously!

Buy Cyber Rants—*you'll be so pleased you did!"*

—Leora Bach, CPA,
Executive Career Coach & Strategist;
Best-Selling Author of *Ace Your C-Suite Interview*

CYBER RANTS

FORBIDDEN SECRETS AND SLIGHTLY EMBELLISHED TRUTHS ABOUT CORPORATE CYBERSECURITY PROGRAMS, FRAMEWORKS AND BEST PRACTICES

MICHAEL ROTONDO   **LAURO CHAVEZ**   **ZACH FULLER**

CYBER RANTS

FORBIDDEN SECRETS AND
SLIGHTLY EMBELLISHED TRUTHS
ABOUT CORPORATE CYBERSECURITY
PROGRAMS, FRAMEWORKS,
AND BEST PRACTICES

Lauro Chavez,
Michael Rotondo,
Zach Fuller

STRATEGIC EDGE INNOVATIONS PUBLISHING
LOS ANGELES, TORONTO, MONTREAL

Copyright © 2020 by **Silent Sector, LLC.** All rights reserved.

No part of this publication may be reproduced, distributed, or transmitted in any form or by any means, including photocopying, recording, or other electronic or mechanical methods, without the prior written permission of the author, except in the case of brief quotations embodied in critical reviews and certain other non-commercial uses permitted by copyright law. For permission requests send an email to Book@CyberRants.com

First Edition. Published by:
Strategic Edge Innovations Publishing
340 S Lemon Ave #2027
Walnut, California 91789-2706
(866) 467-9090
StrategicEdgeInnovations.com

Publisher's Note: The views expressed in this work are solely those of the authors and do not necessarily reflect the views of the publisher, and the publisher hereby disclaims any responsibilities for them.

Editor: Eric D. Groleau

Cover Design: Teslim Dawodu

Cyber Rants / Rotondo, Chavez, Fuller. -- 1st ed.
ISBN: 978-1-7333385-5-4 (Kindle)
ISBN: 978-1-7333385-6-1 (Paperback)

DISCLAIMER

The contents of this book are provided for education and awareness purposes only. This material does not contain all threats, risks, or considerations related to cybersecurity and compliance. The authors, publisher, nor any affiliated entities take no responsibility for the use, practice, or implementation of any material presented, nor provide any guarantees for the material or statements made. Professional advisory and support are recommended for all matters relating to cybersecurity, compliance, and risk management.

ACKNOWLEDGMENTS

We would like to extend our sincerest appreciation to everyone who helped us through our journey of building and growing Silent Sector. We are grateful for our incredible Advisory Board members, Scott Celley, Giselle Chapman, Dale Micetic, and John Nickerson.

Our clients make all of this possible. They are amazing companies made up of even more amazing people, each working to grow, improve, and transform their industries. Every day, they are creating jobs, advancing society, and ultimately making the world a better place. We are grateful to serve you!

We thank our editor and publisher, Eric D. Groleau, for all of his guidance and support as we put our thoughts into words and made them available to the world!

Haidon Storro supported our research and made contributions to both this book and our company. She is an incredibly talented cybersecurity professional, growing in her career with unlimited potential to strengthen our Nation's security posture. Thank you, Haidon!

We thank our network of friends and industry experts for their insight, thought leadership, quotes, and testimonials in this book.

Thanks to all the people doing their best to protect their organizations and our Nation from cyber criminals. Finally, thanks to each of you who take this book to heart and use the information to make the digital world a safer place!

Our highest respect and gratitude,

Michael Rotondo, Lauro Chavez & Zach Fuller

TABLE OF CONTENTS

Praise for Cyber Rants iii
Disclaimer xiii
Acknowledgments xv
Table of Contents xvii
Pre-Rant xxi
Introduction xxiii
Additional Materials & Resources xxvii

FUNDAMENTAL CYBER RANTS 1

CYBERSECURITY AS AN ASSET 7
   Enter the 3rd Party Cybersecurity Questionnaire 8
   What Happens After I Submit a 3rd Party
   Cybersecurity Questionnaire? 10
   What If You Cannot Meet All the Requirements
   in the Security Questionnaire? 11

CYBERSECURITY INDUSTRY CHALLENGES 13
   The People Problem 14
   The Wrong Focus 14
   The Elephant in the Room 15
   Driving On 16

FAIL, ALMOST, NAILED IT! 19

ELEMENTS OF AN EFFECTIVE CYBERSECURITY POSTURE 25

8 STEPS TO IMPLEMENTING YOUR CYBERSECURITY PROGRAM ... 33

IMPLEMENTATION MODELS 45
   DIY Model: Do it Yourself 45
   Hire In-House Cybersecurity Professionals 46
   Managed Security Service Provider (MSSP) Model 48
   Partnered Security Service Provider™ (PSSP) Model 49
   Will an IT Company Cover Our Cybersecurity? 50
   Cybersecurity Expenditures 51
   Implementation Tips 53
   How to Ensure Ongoing Protection 54

EXPERTISE-DRIVEN CYBERSECURITY® **57**
    What the Cybersecurity Industry Can Learn
    from Asymmetrical Warfare 57
    The Elements of Expertise 58
    People > Technology 59
    Case Study: Growing SAAS Company with
    Enterprise Prospects 61

BUILDING AND KEEPING THE TEAM **63**
    What Does an Ideal IT Employee Want? 68
    The Search 71
    Compensation: Show me the Money!!! 75
    The Process 78

WHAT'S IN A PROACTIVE CYBERSECURITY PROGRAM? **85**

BUILDING A SECURITY CONSCIOUS CULTURE **99**
    Rules of a Security Conscious Culture 104

CYBER RISK ASSESSMENTS AND PENETRATION TESTING **105**
    Cyber Risk Assessment vs. Penetration Test 106
    Think Like the Bad Guy 107
    Standards for Cyber Risk Assessments and
    Penetration Testing 108
    Risks of Conducting a Penetration Test
    or Cyber Risk Assessment 112
    What a Penetration Test Should Deliver to You 121
    Penetration Testing Extras That Are "Nice to Have" 121
    What Can You Expect to Pay for a Penetration Test? 123
    Fifty Shades of Pen Test 124
    Manual vs. Automated Penetration Testing Methods 125
    Don't Forget About Physical Penetration Testing 128
    Physical Penetration Testing: Games and Theory 129
    Mechanics of Physical Intrusion 131
    Reaction and Response Protocol Checks for Your Staff 142
    What The Cybercriminals Are up to (Dark Campaigns) 146
    Vulnerability Validation and Re-Ranking Strategy 149
    Advantages and Disadvantages of SIEM 152

CYBERSECURITY COMPLIANCE & FRAMEWORKS **157**
    Cybersecurity Frameworks vs. Cybersecurity Compliance 158
    Common Frameworks 159
        CIS Controls 159
        NIST CSF 160
        NIST SP 800-171 161

      NIST SP 800-53 162
      HITRUST CSF 163
      ISO 27001 164
      ISO 27002 164
      COBIT.. 165
   Common Compliance Standards 166
      PCI-DSS 166
      HIPAA 167
      FINRA 168
      CMMC 169
      SOC 2 170
      SOC for Cybersecurity 170
      SOX 171
      GDPR 172
      FERPA 173
      CCPA 174
   Other State Requirements 174

OPERATIONALIZATION OF COMPLIANCE 177
   Implementing an Operationalized PCI Program 182
   Example: Evidence Matrix for PCI V.3 190

DO YOU REALLY NEED ANOTHER CYBERSECURITY TOOL? 191

REACTIVE DEFENSE VS. PROACTIVE CYBERSECURITY 199

WHERE DO MSPS FIT IN A CYBERSECURITY PROGRAM? 207

FINISHING THE RANT 231

ABOUT SILENT SECTOR 233

ABOUT THE AUTHORS 235

COMMON CYBERSECURITY TERMS TO KNOW 239

ADDITIONAL MATERIALS & RESOURCES 245

PRE-RANT

There seems to be a nearly-continuous stream of headlines in the news exposing yet another major organization, city, county, or regular user falling victim to a cyberattack. Meanwhile, cybersecurity remains one of the most misunderstood requirements of today's business environment. Leaders and their teams struggle to keep up with the changing environment, where security threats are increasing exponentially, in quantity and complexity, while trying to maintain focus on their key roles.

Today's companies are completely reliant on technology. As a result, it is critical that you understand the fundamentals of how and when technology presents risks to your organization. *Cyber Rants* will shed light on the misunderstood risks that have remained in the shadows for far too long.

While building an effective cybersecurity posture may seem daunting at first, the fundamentals and implementation guidance will provide you with clarity for making informed decisions.

Cyber Rants is written in a way that benefits both technical and non-technical organizational leaders and decision makers. This guide is designed to help you speak the language of cybersecurity, regardless of your background. Use it first as a course to gain a foundational understanding of organizational cybersecurity. Then use it as a desk reference to support the security, longevity, and credibility of your organization.

The authors bring over 50 years of combined cybersecurity and IT experience. They have advised and supported U.S.-based companies and government agencies with 30 to 300,000 employees, ranging from startups to banks and healthcare companies, all the way to the United

States Army and NASA. They are the founding partners of Silent Sector, an Arizona-based Expertise-Driven Cybersecurity® services firm serving clients nationwide. Learn more at www.silentsector.com

Silent Sector, LLC
480-447-9658 | info@silentsector.com | www.silentsector.com

INTRODUCTION

If you are holding this book, then it is meant for you. How do we know? It's simple. People don't read cybersecurity books for entertainment, except those of us in the business. We're often described as "a little different" than most. Whether you were offered a copy, you bought it online, or it just appeared on your desk with a thumb drive and no note attached, this book is a keeper (but throw away the thumb drive).

Cyber Rants was written for all those looking to implement a cybersecurity program, improve their current program, or simply learn what is involved in protecting the organization and people they serve. Regardless of your technical background or lack thereof, *Cyber Rants* will take you through a highly productive journey deep into the important topics that most in the industry only gloss over.

Cyber Rants will expose it like it is! We will share the insider information that we wish everyone in the cybersecurity industry would come out and share openly. Transparency is our goal and ranting is our method. Some of our statements will be light-hearted and fun, some will be boring but crucial, and others will be downright harsh; maybe even give you chills. Hang in there though, nobody is pointing fingers... Yet.

The content included in this book was written for very specific reasons. Every word was carefully selected, with the exception of those that were just the writers letting off steam. Leaders of organizations need to know this information because it is critical in the fight against cybercrime.

The authors are pretty cool guys, so they say. They have many years of experience in every topic discussed throughout this book and their cybersecurity services firm, Silent Sector, is protecting mid-market and emerging companies every day. They certainly practice what they preach. We need to start ranting soon, so you can read more about these dudes at the end of the book.

The first fact is, cyber criminals are winning. There is no way to sugarcoat it. We must do more to protect our Nation; where "we" is specifically referring to technical and non-technical business leaders throughout North America.

Companies lose billions of dollars every year to cyber criminals and people of all levels in the corporate hierarchy are being fired after cyber-attacks. This is causing a cascade of resources to be depleted throughout our economy. Only awareness, education, and action, your action, will turn the tides.

But it's not all doom and gloom! Cybersecurity brings major benefits to the organizations that take it seriously.

Effective cybersecurity allows good people to do great things through innovation. Technology must continue to grow and thrive. We want to see technology being used for good, educating people, strengthening worldwide communication, reducing poverty, and saving lives. Cybersecurity is an enabler of that. So yeah… We're pretty much saving the world here.

Cybersecurity will improve operations across entire organizations. The benefits of heightened awareness, attention to detail, clear procedures, and empowerment to respond to threats will strengthen culture in a way that spreads far beyond IT and security operations.

When approached effectively, cybersecurity also increases revenue and profitability. Cybersecurity provides credibility, longevity, and a competitive advantage in today's business environment. We want you to experience how cybersecurity can be an asset within your organization and how to leverage it to maximize your success. We've seen it play a major role in helping clients gain millions of dollars' worth of contracts. If they can do it, you can do it.

If you're hoping for a fluffy, romantic feel-good novel with a great storyline, this book will be a severe disappointment. While it sounds wonderful to obtain the benefits of cybersecurity and sleep well at night,

INTRODUCTION

nothing happens without action. We're about to get down to serious business here. When information is repeated, it's because it is that important. It's also so you can pick up this book and quickly reference the information you need as you're in the process of building a strong security program.

Read through the principles presented in early chapters to gain a strong understanding of proactive cybersecurity fundamentals. We'll give you industry insight, share what is important and what is not, reveal ways to build a security program, and share some real-world examples.

The later sections of this book are for everyone wanting to do more than dip their toe in the water. This is where it gets deep and meaty. We'll cover topics like penetration testing, compliance, and share more of what the industry won't tell you about products and services. Don't worry, none of the information requires you to have a PhD from MIT, just a decent attitude and desire to learn.

Love it, hate it, rant back, or be indifferent. Regardless, there is at least one gold nugget in here for everyone. Leaders and decision makers will use it as a desk reference for anything that applies to their organization now, or for issues that come up in the future.

Most importantly, don't wait to take action. Implement what you learn and start having conversations with other organizational leaders. Whatever you do, just do something to get the ball rolling. As you move forward, you'll gain momentum and the approach for your organization will start to become clear. With the right mindset and people to call on for expertise, your proactive cybersecurity program will start to take shape.

You'll discover our "Rants" throughout this book. While these are opinions, they are declarations of the authors which are so strong, they might as well be considered unwavering, inalienable truths, etched in stone, backed up to the cloud and the secret thumb drive that stays in the fireproof gun safe… Truths that have always been and will always be.

Sometimes it takes a rant to drive a point home, so feel free to rant back to the world anything you've discovered in this book. After all, Cyber Rants are for everyone's good if they protect people from cyber criminals.

On special occasions, you'll also find Ancient Infosec Proverbs. Each Ancient Infosec Proverb encourages an extended pause and deeper reflection. Don't be afraid to go to a quiet room and meditate on it. After all, one who takes the Ancient Infosec Proverb to heart will surely prosper with strong defense and great honor among cyber warriors.

We truly hope you enjoy *Cyber Rants*. More importantly, we hope you put the information to good use by supporting the development of a proactive cybersecurity program for the organization that you serve.

Cyber Rants was written for the amazing people serving organizations, large and small, across our great Nation. It was written to equip you with the fundamental knowledge to protect your organization as you step into this fight against cybercrime.

Our vision is that one day, companies in North America will become known as the hardest targets of any in the world, causing cyber criminals to take their schemes elsewhere.

We cannot accomplish this alone. You are a critical part of that vision. We wish you happiness and success. Enjoy *Cyber Rants* and reach out to us if you need some extra support or if you just want to rant!

www.CyberRants.com | book@cyberrants.com

ADDITIONAL MATERIALS & RESOURCES

Access your Additional Materials & Resources referenced throughout this book at
http://resources.cyberrants.com

FUNDAMENTAL CYBER RANTS

Let the rants begin! We'll start by covering our core beliefs which have developed through years of work, study, mentorship, teaching, and lessons learned the hard way.

Cybersecurity Is More Than Just Technology

Cybersecurity, at its most successful, is a combination of technology, process, compliance, and effective end user training. The most expensive firewall in the world won't install, configure, and manage itself. Without a compliance framework, we may be just guessing at what we need to secure the enterprise and potentially missing critical components. Without process, there is no control over an enterprise's change and growth. Without a trained and motivated staff with effective leadership, technology, process, and compliance are worthless. In many cases, a single user who can't identify a phishing email can potentially bring down the whole house of cards.

Technology Is Not the Problem

Technology is not to blame for cybercrime; people are. Technology merely provides cybercriminals with a means to commit crime. Technology must be embraced, leveraged, and continuously improved. Those not embracing technology are quickly falling behind in every industry. The weakest link is always going to be the humans using the technology. This is why training is so critical to the effective use of technology. Industry standards recommend interactive security awareness training annually and as soon as possible when onboarding new employees. Silent Sector believes, based on our experience, that training needs to be quarterly at a minimum to account for current threats like phishing, smishing, or social engineering as well as a renewal of cybersecurity fundamentals. The need to maintain effective cybersecurity awareness among team members is now a permanent part of business operations.

Cybersecurity Is Not a Loss

In the current evolving world of technology, it is clear that cybersecurity process, planning, and compliance are now requirements of doing business. With the proliferation of new compliance requirements and certifications, such as SOC, PCI, CMMC, NIST, ISO, and others, becoming part of the vendor onboarding process, not to mention the venture capital process, cybersecurity maturity can be a significant competitive advantage. For proactive organizations, cybersecurity is what sets their company apart from the competitors by removing roadblocks and accelerating the sales process. There is no way to argue that an organization can save money in the short term by having minimal security measures or none at all. When considering the costs of a single breach, an effective cybersecurity program will significantly increase the bottom line over the lifetime of an organization.

Cybersecurity Is Not a One-Time Task

Efficient cybersecurity is built over time and must be maintained. In short, you cannot achieve a certain level of protection and then let your security efforts go dormant. Cybersecurity maturity is a continuously evolving process. Technology constantly evolves and so do vulnerabilities, threats, and risks. No single technology or quick fix will ensure an organization's protection indefinitely.

IT and Cybersecurity Are Separate yet Complementary Disciplines

Effective security cannot be considered the sole responsibility of IT professionals. To be effective, cybersecurity and IT professionals work together to support the greater good of the organization. While technology is certainly a component of cybersecurity, it is important to note that their practitioners differ from core IT staff. Security professionals are highly specialized in their skillset and focus. It is incumbent on operational and security management to support each other to ensure the strongest possible security posture for the enterprise. The Keep the Lights On (KTLO) IT Team and the Cybersecurity Team should learn from each other and continuously increase their combined capabilities in support of those they serve.

Everyone Is Responsible for Security

We all use technology, and that technology can be used against us. Therefore, cybersecurity is the responsibility of every individual. It is critical that a comprehensive training program should be required of all enterprise users, no matter how small the enterprise. Online training classes can be purchased for minimal cost and will, at least, provide your team with a basic insight into cybersecurity. It is also important to understand that someone else's unprotected technologies can be used to abuse others, whether or not they have any relation to you or your organization. The cyber hygiene of your vendors is also critical to the security and stability of your operations. Don't go through the trouble of training your users, securing your enterprise and then leave an unprotected backdoor from a careless vendor.

Effective Cyber Security Does Not Hinder Operations

Proactive cybersecurity will help improve business operations, even beyond technical and compliance matters. With properly communicated, documented, and enforced processes, cybersecurity becomes an asset that functions seamlessly with daily operations.

Effective processes will not only standardize how a company operates, they will also ensure that any modifications to the company's computing environment are committed. It is important to follow a standard change management process that will ensure that updates to the environment don't lead to unintended consequences. These include insecure or undocumented firewall ports, vendor connections that don't adhere to your standards of cybersecurity, lack of communication between business units, or additional risk being introduced into the environment.

Compliance Is Not Security

Achieving compliance to a specific standard (i.e., NIST, HIPAA, PCI DSS, or SOC 2) is positively answering the question, *"do we meet these standard criteria?"* Cybersecurity is a comprehensive approach to answer, *"where are our risks and what is our plan to minimize the risks?"* In other words, you can be compliant but not secure. However, if you are secure, you are more than likely covering your compliance requirements.

The standards imposed by governing bodies are not always all-encompassing. Sadly, many organizations only consider compliance to be a once-a-year activity, which turns into a 90-day fire drill to check off a box on a list, only to make auditors happy and satisfy industry requirements. The compliance, operations, and cybersecurity teams need to work together to ensure that an enterprise is compliant and secure. Unfortunately, many companies either can't afford the three teams or don't understand why they need the all three teams, considering the cost. Most simply work to take care of the KTLO tasks with an operations team, either expecting the KTLO team to manage security and compliance. Others will bring in consultants once a year to manage the compliance piece. In this case, they still miss the critical security piece. As technology evolves, so does the threat vector and attack surface for cyber criminals. Cybersecurity must be addressed as part of standard operations and staffed internally, or least engage a security services company to develop and maintain a security program for the organization.

Rant On!

Above we have listed what we consider to be important fundamental beliefs about cybersecurity. Moving forward, with these core principles, we will explain in greater depth why cybersecurity is a practice that involves not only IT professionals, but anyone who touches a computer at home or at work.

CYBERSECURITY AS AN ASSET

What if we told you that cybersecurity will accelerate your company's ability to get new customers and keep them longer? What if you could land that next large enterprise clients you've been hoping for, simply by leveraging cybersecurity as your competitive advantage? Would you strongly consider implementing a proactive cybersecurity program?

Hold that thought. Let's face it, we've all heard about the big breaches like Target and Home Depot. You have to ask yourself, *"Should I be trusting this business with my payment information?"* Well, for most Americans, the answer was *"yes"* because not only did the organization do a great job of responding and addressing customer protection, but they corrected the problem and moved forward with cybersecurity being top of mind.

Of course, there is the fact we all still needed a place to shop locally but imagine if there was a place just like Target called "Barget" and it was almost the exact same company as Target, but used a blue colored signage and had strong security for their technologies. If Barget advertised the benefits of their strengthened security in their commercials, would you have stopped shopping at Target after their breach and given your business to Barget instead?

Many consumers switch to other brands after news of a breach, even when they experience little to no inconvenience themselves. The effect is exponentially greater in business-to-business (B2B) scenarios where the ramifications of a vendor's breach can cost millions.

When breaches occur, companies lose their brand integrity. We feel like those companies have neglected to protect their business systems, the same systems handling our personal data. Our feelings are justified because in most cases, the companies being breached have been negligent to some extent.

Cybersecurity, rather the act of hardening technology assets, their humans and core business functions, has not always been a major business priority. Companies are known to think of cybersecurity initiatives as "extremely expensive" and make excuses like, *"it's not necessarily because we don't have anything that cybercriminals would want."* Sure, an in-house cybersecurity staff can be expensive and even with the cost-saving option of outsourcing it, those services can still be pricey. Still, that's no excuse to not adopt a basic cybersecurity mindset, which costs nothing. Furthermore, the ultimate cost of failing to implement appropriate cybersecurity measures is far greater than building a proactive security program. Just ask Target or Home Depot!

Cybersecurity questionnaires are now a standard part of the B2B sales process. Companies that want to grow and win contracts with enterprise clients must be able to complete cybersecurity questionnaires in a way that presents them as a viable vendor with a low level of risk. Security vetting stops enterprise sales in its tracks. Sales people hate it but leadership knows it's necessary. Like it or not, it's better to be prepared to answer security questionnaires than to resist and miss major revenue opportunities as a result.

ENTER THE 3RD PARTY CYBERSECURITY QUESTIONNAIRE

Adopting a cybersecurity mindset will be critical moving forward as the business paradigm on this issue is increasing its reach. Some of you reading this book might be in the early stages of building new tech ventures while others will have leadership roles in very large companies that are beginning to implement cybersecurity measures as an organization. In either case, at some point you will encounter a "security questionnaire" from one of your potential customers, business partners, capital sources, or insurance companies. Maybe you have already received a few.

Today, Target has a large cybersecurity team and loads of mature processes to protect business transaction and their own corporate assets. Part of that cybersecurity team probably includes a Risk and Governance group. It would be the responsibility that group to figure out a way to validate the security posture for all 3rd parties that Target may be doing business with, from manufacturing and shipping, to the consultants and technology platforms that they may be using. Risk and governance teams will typically assess vendor risk by using a 3rd-party security questionnaire.

Most large organizations have created their own 3rd party security questionnaire, which they send out before signing any deals with vendors or partners. This document, usually a spreadsheet, will have anywhere from 15 to over 300 cybersecurity-related questions. The complexity of the document will depend on the organization and maturity of their processes.

Many of the larger companies will direct you to an online portal to answer their security questionnaire. It is a requirement to complete these questionnaires in order to gain their business and you will always notice a few common standardized questions. One of them being, *"have you received a 3rd party penetration test for your services?"* If the answer is *"yes,"* they usually want you to upload/provide the cover sheet (as the internal contents would be highly confidential and dangerous to share with non-internal staff) or an attestation letter of testing from the 3rd party that conducted your penetration test. They may also ask you for your penetration testing score card, which would also demonstrate that your current risk posture was validated by a 3rd party. Another common question is regarding the at-rest and in-transit security mechanisms being used. Companies want to know details in their questionnaires. For example, if you are using SQL for data management, can you confirm that you have TDE enabled and to what extent? Likewise, if you offer a web solution or service, expect questions about transmission security details, credentials for storage, OWASP Top 10 testing, development processes, all things SDLC, etc.

WHAT HAPPENS AFTER I SUBMIT A 3ᴿᴰ PARTY CYBERSECURITY QUESTIONNAIRE?

Simple. A team of people will rank your business services as low risk or high risk. This will essentially depend on how many questions you could answer effectively and what evidence was provided to support your answers. If your organization is considered high risk, they will probably go with a competitor in your market that has cybersecurity top of mind and therefore, presents a low level of risk. Your answers on these questionnaires go back to the risk and governance team, which will review them and give your company an internal risk rating. They will base their review on their perception of the specific security control requirements that your organization has in place and what security control requirements you might not have yet.

Based on the determined risk level, the security team may advise the organization not to participate in your company's service offering, due to the risk of impacting their business integrity, their current security compliance posture, or both.

The Lexus Nexus breach has taught us that we can't trust 3ʳᵈ parties to integrate securely on their own. Organizations have to develop their own security requirements sheet and provide it to their vendors or other appropriate parties. There must be a requirement for foundational cybersecurity standards to protect operations between business entities.

Even if you indicate that you are road-mapping something like "at rest encryption" on the questionnaire, you will still be flagged for follow-ups at regular intervals if the customer chooses your services. Expect to deliver progress reports every three months for any items that you have identified as "in the works."

It is also important to understand that security questionnaires tend to cover cybersecurity measures across an entire organization. This is because companies want to understand all the areas where their suppliers may be vulnerable and identify risk factors that could hinder larger operations in the event of a breach.

For example, the Payment Card Industry Data Security Standard (PCI DSS) was developed specifically to protect credit card transactions and offered us section 12.8.4 (Maintain a program to monitor service providers' PCI DSS compliance status at least annually). A company could build a program to monitor only the PCI DSS compliance status of their service providers. However, from an enterprise risk perspective, focusing risk management specifically toward credit card transactions would be covering only a fraction of the risk presented by the company's 3rd party suppliers. A narrow-focused approach like this would be considered negligent, as it would fail to account for most of the risk factors.

WHAT IF YOU CANNOT MEET ALL THE REQUIREMENTS IN THE SECURITY QUESTIONNAIRE?

When a potential vendor or business service provider cannot answer all of the requirements on a company's security questionnaire, the typical approach is to find similar vendors that can show better operational security. The risk evaluation would indicate the vendor that can fulfill the needs, while meeting all security requirements. Putting your organization in position to quickly answer security questionnaires from potential clients should now be at the top of the list for future endeavors. As cybersecurity continues to gain importance for executive teams and boards of directors, risky vendors will not be considered.

Companies know when their vendor's cybersecurity questionnaire responses are a load of baloney! Bad answers on a security questionnaire are not worth losing a current or prospective contract.

Companies seeking growth and larger customers must be prepared to work for the next level of organization. These ideal prospects are actively keeping cybersecurity top of mind and integrated into daily business operations. Having great cybersecurity hygiene will allow your growing company to be ready with the right documents and attestations proving your strong cybersecurity program. The ability to provide this information to prospects will demonstrate an increased organizational maturity level which becomes a credibility builder and competitive advantage.

When prospects see that your company puts the same emphasis on cybersecurity as theirs, it eliminates what would otherwise be a bottleneck in the sales process while encouraging larger engagements.

Companies also benefit from increased brand reputation and client trust. After all, why would strong clients risk doing business with anyone else after you have demonstrated year after year that you continuously protect their organization as you would your own?

CYBERSECURITY INDUSTRY CHALLENGES

Cybersecurity is a young industry, relatively to others. It is still taking shape and companies are racing to gain market share. Some of the world's top minds are working tirelessly to stay ahead of threats and protect our economy.

Unfortunately, and there's no way to "sugar coat" it, the cybersecurity industry is failing to protect mid-market and emerging companies in the United States. Why?

Without focused expertise and guidance, companies struggle to understand and keep up with changing compliance requirements, evolving threats, and workforce challenges. Meanwhile, complexity and costs continue to rise.

Let's stop blaming our Nation's cybersecurity problems on the shortage of security professionals. In war, you accomplish the mission with the resources you have, not the ones you wish you had.

Most people are quick to blame the shortage of cybersecurity professionals in the United States, citing studies showing massive numbers of unfulfilled security positions. While our Nation struggles to keep up with the demand for technical talent, there are other, mostly overlooked, issues contributing to many of the Nation's cybersecurity struggles.

THE PEOPLE PROBLEM

There is a severe issue of underutilization and misutilization of our existing cybersecurity professionals. Speaking with security professionals across the country, we hear almost unanimously, *"I spend so much time in meetings and navigating company politics that I'm left with almost no time to do the work that needs to be done to protect the company."*

In other words, cyber professionals know what needs to be done to protect their organizations but must constantly fight to get the support they need to fulfill their duties. Time wasted in meetings and navigating politics quickly turns into frustrated security professionals looking for new jobs with better working environments.

Combined with the talent shortage, this frustration is causing most companies to struggle with retention of their cybersecurity professionals. It is now common for security professionals to change employers every 1–2 years. This rate of turnover creates a tremendous expense for any organization.

In today's competitive hiring landscape, organizations must understand how to attract and retain their technical professionals, a topic which we will discuss in detail later in this book.

THE WRONG FOCUS

In addition to the talent struggle, the cybersecurity industry is placing an overwhelming emphasis on the development of new tools and technologies. Building a new security tool or technology has a strong allure from a business perspective, to the point of creating a modern-day Gold Rush. Venture capital and other investment money is being thrown at cybersecurity technology companies, almost blindly in some cases, with high hopes of "hockey stick earnings" and an exit at a massive multiple of revenue. Of course, most of these ventures never get off the ground for a variety of reasons.

More importantly, cybersecurity professionals know that technology alone does little to stop cyberattacks. Technology will not win this fight without the human expertise to properly plan and implement solutions. Effective cybersecurity requires expert practitioners. Those professionals are the "boots on the ground," doing the work to minimize cyber risk.

Cybersecurity is not about technology; it is about people. Tools and technology are important and we should always continue to innovate. We must maintain the upper hand and develop advanced capabilities to do so. However, let us not forget the fact that the vast majority of cyber-attacks are a result of human error and oversight. Most attacks are preventable with proper planning and security measures implemented by cybersecurity professionals.

Whether it might be due to employees' lack of awareness, misconfigured technologies, or a lack of decision by the leadership team to implement a security program, the human element is both the primary problem and solution in the fight against cybercrime.

We believe in using a technology-agnostic approach. It is important to develop a holistic security strategy and maximize the capabilities of what your organization already has in place, before investing in new technologies. More to come on Expertise-Driven Cybersecurity® in later chapters.

THE ELEPHANT IN THE ROOM

How do we build a holistic security posture with limited resources when a new "compliance requirement of the week" keeps popping up?

The problem with compliance requirements is that they are typically focused on a single aspect of protection; yet they can take an overwhelming amount of time to achieve and maintain. Companies are regularly faced with the dilemma of postponing proactive security measures to meet federal, state, and industry requirements.

For example, requirements such as General Data Protection Regulation (GDPR) and California Consumer Privacy Act (CCPA) focus on Personally Identifiable Information (PII). The protection of personal information is definitely important but it does little to ensure an organization's ability to operate. While companies divert resources to focus on meeting compliance requirements, they are often left susceptible to attacks which can render the company inoperable. Nobody wins in this scenario and tremendous economic damage is incurred.

A perfect solution does not exist and this dilemma is likely to continue for many years. However, the key concept should be to make an industry-recognized security framework the center of your security program and then work on compliance as needed.

Focus efforts on aligning to an industry-recognized security framework first and the achievement of compliance requirements will happen much quicker.

Some of industry recognized security frameworks include NIST SP 800-171, NIST SP 800-53, CIS Controls, and ISO 27001. Each of these is covered in greater detail in this book. The important point is that these are a holistic list of items that should be in place for a company to be considered as having a robust and effective cybersecurity program.

As a company aligns to a cybersecurity framework, it becomes much easier to show conformance with a variety of security compliance requirements. With an effective security posture, a company can follow the steps outlined in the later chapter discussing Operationalization of Compliance. This will make compliance achievable year-over-year while minimizing the burden on internal and external resources.

DRIVING ON

While the cybersecurity industry is still young and figuring itself out, one fact is certain. Cybersecurity is now a business requirement that is here to stay. No amount of technology, compliance, or other regulations will fix this. It will take the continuous effort of organizational leadership, staff, and cybersecurity professionals to minimize risk and react to the uncertainties to come. The sooner we embrace this direction as individual companies and as a Nation, the quicker we'll establish proactive security measures and the more successful we'll all be as we grow into our technology-centric world.

FAIL, ALMOST, NAILED IT!

A mature cybersecurity practice gives you a competitive advantage over others in your industry. We see proof of this on a continual basis, especially with business-to-business (B2B) organizations seeking large-enterprise clients. We will now discuss cases where cybersecurity is impacting sales pipelines. These are case studies and amalgams of first-hand accounts, some directly from Silent Sector clients and others that the team members have experienced elsewhere.

Cybersecurity can be a vicious rollercoaster for those who let it; taking one to the highest emotional peaks and lowest valleys of despair. Hang in there, like a low-frequency radio wave—stay calm with a low amplitude, and you'll travel far.

Fail

Why start with the fail? This simply highlights an example of how a lack of commitment and basic knowledge of cybersecurity becomes a major issue for an organization. Unfortunately, this is not just a one-off experience. This happens every day. Cybersecurity is not a box to be checked, but rather a commitment to a company and the people it serves.

Company 1: A venture capital (VC) funded startup software company with a few hundred employees was dealing with large Fortune 100 companies to provide a SaaS solution for each customer's internal staff. The software company did not store any personally identifiable information (PII) data other than name and email address for login purposes. Because of this, data and cybersecurity were never part of their original development plans. Their SaaS infrastructure was 100% cloud-based. Their "enterprise" consisted of geographically dispersed development resources and development staff outsourced overseas. In short, they needed a full-security review of the enterprise, not just an analysis of their application. Due to time-to-market concerns, they were focusing on building the best product they could deliver. Security had taken a backseat to expedite development, an all too common occurrence among SaaS companies.

With only a vague understanding of application and enterprise security, they engaged multiple "security" companies, which provided pretty graphs and documents, which, in turn, were provided to their customers. These automated outputs do nothing but let their customer "check the box" on the list to indicate that the application is secure, without sufficient evaluation. There was no true commitment to security. Due to running lean, with only a small development team, there were no internal or external resources to properly manage security.

As their market expanded to larger companies, security suddenly became critical to grow. When larger prospects were asking real security questions, the software company engaged a true cybersecurity firm with a commitment to securing the enterprise. However, due to executive management's lack of commitment to cybersecurity, the budget was severely restricted and the appropriate amount of service could not be provided.

The software company's leadership disregarded the guidance from the security company. Without commitment from leadership, they reverted to trying to convince the prospective clients with pretty graphs and automated reports in an attempt to simply, "check the security box." This approach put the security company in a corner as they refused to imply that the software company's environment was properly secured. Meanwhile, the sales pipeline was bottlenecked since prospective clients were not gaining confidence in the security posture of the platform.

In short, they had no true understanding about what the implementation of enterprise-wide security entailed. They started to realize that this was not a simple box to check on a list. Instead of embracing the reality of the situation, they tried to bypass what was required and focus only on what it took to look secure, in an attempt to close the next sale. This ultimately ended in frustration, failure, lost revenue, time and irreparable damage to the software company's reputation. They ultimately failed, despite having a good product, due to their unwillingness to meet industry (and client) security standards and requirements.

When an organization acts like they have a security program just to "check a box," without taking it seriously, the long-term costs become overbearing and people get fired.

Almost

A venture capital (VC) funded startup software company was serving Fortune 100 companies to provide a unique data management solution. They didn't store any PII data. Since they did not store any data, security was not part of their product roadmap until a large customer asked them to provide an overview of their security posture.

The document requested was unlike anything the team had seen before. The team, comprised of marketing, sales, and developers, was lost but did not want to lose this sale since it could be a 'make it or break it' situation for the company. Rather than faking the responses on the document (like Ugly above), they engaged a cybersecurity services firm, Silent Sector. Cybersecurity professionals walked them through the security questionnaire and provided guidance on how to respond to these requests in the future. The deal closed in a timely manner and the company began to grow. This was a partial win for security in the short term. Unfortunately, security is still not a requirement for them due to tight funding, something common for early-stage companies. This may come back to haunt them as it is much more painful to implement security once a company is established than at the early stages where it can be baked into processes and culture.

Imperfect action always beats perfect inaction! You have to start somewhere and sometimes that starting point is not ideal. However, doing something is better than nothing, so long as you're serious about continuous improvement.

Nailed It!

A mid-size technology implementation company that specialized in a well-known enterprise platform has been doing a fantastic job of getting new clients and closing deals. This was largely because of their homebrew fashion of working within their specialty. As they began to grow, they started chasing larger prospective clients. When the larger prospects became interested in the smaller company's services, they started to send detailed security questionnaires. These questionnaires included items the technology company was not doing and had not yet considered. Required tasks, like vulnerability scanning, penetration testing, incident response, data protection, and leadership for a cybersecurity program, were not part of their standard operations. The lack of these practices caused a bottleneck in the sales process when the large prospects began to postpone the signing of deals, while waiting for responses to the security questionnaires. Those companies started to take their business elsewhere, due to the slow response and lack of almost every cybersecurity measure required of their vendors.

Change happened quickly when the CFO was made aware of a new client, potentially signing on a one-million-dollar contract. The CFO noticed that a few large deals failed to close due to questions about cybersecurity practices. He was ready to close the gap to get big profits rolling in. The CFO began to ask questions to the head of Information Technology. Being only a two-person IT shop, they had not been able to do much to address anything related to cybersecurity. They were busy, making sure their staff had hardware and system access to perform their work for clients. They realized that they could not handle security questions internally and began to contact cybersecurity companies for help.

This million-dollar deal was sitting on the edge of the table when they contacted our team at Silent Sector. The CFO made it clear to us that the company was committed to adopting a security mindset to better protect themselves and their customers. He wanted all cybersecurity priorities adopted and implemented immediately.

We were quickly able to assess what the organization had in its toolbox and found that with a minimum investment into the existing tools, we could dramatically improve the security posture across the organization and also get closer to meeting compliance goals. In the first two weeks, and in parallel with other operations, the entire cybersecurity library was built and security awareness training was deployed to the internal teams. Acting as our client's cybersecurity partner, we provided virtual CISO capabilities that included leadership, road-mapping for compliance, continual training, continual scanning and the implementation of a security framework (CIS), all in under 6 months. After conducting penetration testing, we were better able to help the client properly secure their technologies.

Silent Sector was able to speak to the large prospect's CISO (remember the million-dollar deal?) and provide a letter of attestation about security of services and observations. The CISO thanked our team and released the hold on the deal. Our client continues to use our services and they are still successfully obtaining new large enterprise clients, without any bottlenecks in the sales process. They were, in fact, so successful that they were recently acquired for many millions of dollars by a large prominent technology company. It has been an absolute pleasure to help the company adopt a good security doctrine and achieve significant success. They took security seriously, not only to grow revenue, but because it was the right thing to do.

It's so refreshing to work with companies that understand the importance of cybersecurity and make the decision to be proactive. Unfortunately, those companies are still rare.

ELEMENTS OF AN EFFECTIVE CYBERSECURITY POSTURE

Every effective security plan contains the same fundamental components. While specific technologies, processes, procedures, and implementation techniques vary, the following elements must be in place. This is a high-level overview of those elements.

If you have the responsibility for cybersecurity in your organization but don't come from a technical background, don't let it bother you. Cybersecurity is a team effort so don't get too caught up in the details and feel like you need to know everything. Instead, focus your time on finding and leveraging technical experts you trust. Understand the fundamentals of cybersecurity so you can ask better questions, get better answers and make better decisions.

1. Clarity of Purpose

It is critical that an organization's team members clearly understand the "why" behind their cybersecurity efforts. They need to understand what and whom the company needs to protect, both legally and ethically. They should be able to answer the question, *"Why is cybersecurity critical to our company?"*

2. Leadership Support and Recognition of the Topic

The perfect plan and implementation will eventually fail without the buy-in and support of organizational leadership and senior management. Leaders have the highest risk of exposure to targeted attacks and many fall victim to "spear phishing" or other cybercriminal schemes. This is why effective security starts with the support of executives and board members who can lead by example. Non-leadership staff may believe their own security awareness is not as important as leadership, however, based on the law of numbers, the non-leadership staff provide a much larger attack surface for cyber criminals. Therefore, this essential topic should be recognized throughout the organization.

3. Established Security Baseline

An effective plan to improve in any security area starts with understanding your current posture. Establishing this clarity starts with assessing and testing your current security measures, or better yet, engaging a third party to perform the review. This includes technical aspects, such as web presence, network infrastructure and governance components, such as policy and procedures, and your staff's awareness of threats.

An Enterprise Cyber Risk Assessment is a comprehensive picture of your organization's cyber risk exposure. It is a compilation of multiple tests and assessments that identify vulnerabilities, or "attack surfaces," on the critical components that your organization requires to operate.

A penetration test is usually a major component of the Enterprise Cyber Risk Assessment. This test involves leveraging the same tools and techniques that a cybercriminal would use to exploit your network and application technologies. Penetration tests can also include a test of the vulnerabilities that exist around human factors. This is often called "social engineering" or "human hacking." Testing your staff's awareness is important because cybercriminals know that the quickest way into an organization is often through the exploitation of well-meaning but unaware people.

A review of your company's policy and procedure documentation is necessary to prevent potential risks in daily operations. Documentation review is especially critical when an organization is required to be

ELEMENTS OF AN EFFECTIVE CYBERSECURITY POSTURE

compliant under one or more frameworks. Third-party review of your policy documentation can serve as an audit to ensure that you are following the processes as they are written. Policy and process documentation should be reviewed annually to ensure that it still meets the needs of the enterprise.

Clearly defining and understanding the results of thorough testing and assessment lays the foundation for risk reduction.

4. Planning for Continuous Improvement

An effective cybersecurity plan supports the greater needs and initiatives of the organization. Every company should strive to minimize risk on an ongoing basis. This requires promoting the continued development of your internal team's knowledge and capabilities. Even when cybersecurity activities are handled primarily by an outside party, it is important to have one or more in-house team members who act as liaisons between your company and the third-party security service provider because risk can never be fully transferred to a third party.

Measurable goals and benchmarks come in many forms, including an ever-increasing number of compliance frameworks. Most internal goals and benchmarks focus on reducing the total number of vulnerabilities, whereas compliance frameworks require an engagement of the enterprise as a whole. With professional support, organizations can also place financial metrics on vulnerabilities. Knowing the dollar value of cybersecurity creates enormous clarity and allows leadership to understand the costs of specific exposures.

When your organization sets specific goals and benchmarks, include both technical and non-technical matters. For example, you might set goals to reduce external network vulnerabilities by 10% per month and increase the average staff awareness testing score by 15% per quarter.

5. Effective Oversight and Leadership

A strong security program requires oversight and leadership from experienced practitioners and a firm commitment from senior management, who ultimately own the risk for the enterprise. If any of your internal team members have cybersecurity experience that can be used to support your security initiatives, you already have some in-house expertise that can reduce costs and support your efforts. Having an internal team member, even an inexperienced one, who can act as a liaison to a third party will help streamline your cybersecurity initiatives.

As leaders, we all need to trust the experts we hire! If we don't, we're simply wasting time and money only to find ourselves at fault when incidents begin to occur. If we can't trust someone, we shouldn't hire them in the first place just to fill a role, or we need to get rid of them if they're already on the team.

If you have limited to no in-house expertise, you'll want to consult an outside party. Finding the right cybersecurity service provider is like finding any good vendor. The best is to hire a company whose primary function is cybersecurity. You can validate this through client references, certifications, and judging whether their team is a cultural fit to work with your organization.

If you find a company promoting cybersecurity services and the first thing they try to sell you is the "latest and greatest" tool or software, beware! Also, beware if they promote their company as a jack of all trades in technology. You should be cautious of the generalist IT company or managed service provider (MSP) acting as a cybersecurity vendor. While, perhaps with good intentions, their primary objective may be to sell tools you can't support or fully deploy, or additional services like a Security Operations Center (SOC). These are high-margin commoditized offerings that may not necessarily make sense for your organization, despite how great they sound in the sales presentation.

Due to the shortage of qualified cybersecurity firms and resources, it has become a common and dangerous trend for MSPs to offer cybersecurity services, most often a SOC, which is a third party that manages a mixture of hardware and software solutions to monitor events in your environment, and notify you when there is an issue. While a SOC isn't a bad thing and can be an asset when used properly, it is not the answer to all security issues as many in the industry would imply.

6. Company Wide Training and Awareness Testing

People are generally the most vulnerable and exploitable element of a company's cybersecurity posture. Cybercriminals leverage social engineering or human hacking to gather information in support of their cyberattacks. These techniques must be understood to be recognized.

It is wise to implement a consistent staff-awareness training and testing program throughout the entire organization that covers topics such as phishing (malicious email) and smishing (malicious text messages). Physical penetration testing is also a critical, yet often overlooked, part of staff training.

> *"Never trust messages from those you do not know and place great suspicion on messages from those you do know."*
> —Ancient InfoSec Proverb

While it sounds like regular training might take attention away from other critical initiatives, the training process can be automated to provide brief reminders and tests, rather than a single drawn-out educational event. There are a few outstanding training and testing platforms that cover most needs at a very low cost. On a final note on this topic, compliance frameworks are now requiring attestation of training as a requirement to be compliant.

7. Documented Policies and Tracking

In today's environment, a strong security posture is insufficient on its own. Your security policies and procedures must be documented and followed. A cybersecurity policy library should contain a complete set of documents describing how your organization uses technology securely. These documents range from non-technical topics, such as the frequency for creating new user passwords, to technical topics, such as the process for testing and applying critical security patches across the company's network. These policies can be purchased online and customized with significant time and thought process. Or you can have a third party write them for you if your team doesn't have the bandwidth to do it. It is, however, essential to customize policies for your organization, especially when it comes to defining responsible parties and the responsible, accountable, consulted, and informed (RACI) for incident response and disaster recovery. These policies are worthless unless they are accepted and followed. Therefore, it is critical for your enterprise to implement consequences for failures to comply with the policies.

Review and update your cybersecurity policy library, at least annually, or whenever significant changes occur.

8. Recurring Review and Assessment

Cybersecurity is a continuous process. Technologies constantly change, and new exploits are identified daily. Effective cybersecurity includes continuous vulnerability identification to determine new areas of risk. Vulnerability identification includes the scanning and patching of technological risks, penetration testing (both application and physical), and a testing review of your company's standards, policies, and procedures.

ELEMENTS OF AN EFFECTIVE CYBERSECURITY POSTURE

It is advisable to create a regular schedule for risk assessment and penetration testing. These activities should be conducted annually at a minimum. Technology-based companies, such as those who create software and IoT devices, should conduct these tests at least every quarter.

Recurring assessments of your cybersecurity initiatives and security posture will allow your organization to track its progress and understand whether it is allocating resources effectively.

> *"Cybersecurity changes are as sure as the changing of seasons. Over time, one learns to anticipate and work in a state of continuous change."*
> —Ancient InfoSec Proverb

8 STEPS TO IMPLEMENTING YOUR CYBERSECURITY PROGRAM

1. Obtain Leadership's Support.

Senior level leadership support, including the board of directors and C-level executives, is critical to successfully implement anything new or to make significant changes in an organization. A cybersecurity program will touch every part of your enterprise. Prior to implementation, it is critical to discuss the topic with the executive team and leadership. Additionally, it is important to communicate with leadership that there is a direct financial correlation between vulnerabilities and risk. Too often, people unfamiliar with IT security will see the cost of a risk assessment and decide that they would rather assume the risk than pay to reduce it. Inevitably, this approach ends with terrible consequences, costing many times more to fix the mess after a breach, as opposed to being proactive before a breach. Everyone must understand why cybersecurity is important and recognize the potential impact to the enterprise as a whole.

Accept cybersecurity or do not. There is no middle ground. If you choose accept it, support it with respect and an appropriate budget.

When leadership agrees to the implementation of a cybersecurity plan and sets goals, you have a good opportunity to establish your Clarity and Purpose Statement. This document should be presented to the entire enterprise, through leadership's communication channels, be it email, company meeting, or intranet portal.

A leadership meeting is a good time to start discussing your organization's current security posture.

> *For a copy of our Cybersecurity Considerations Guide for Executives and Board Members, visit* http://resources.cyberrants.com/. ***This non-technical document outlines the appropriate questions to ask for a high-level self-assessment.***

2. Understand Current Risks and Vulnerabilities.

Industry best practices recommend that organizations conduct a full Enterprise Cyber Risk Assessment on an annual basis to understand where their technical and human vulnerabilities exist, the accuracy of the disaster and incident recovery process, the status of their security training program, the potential financial loss exposure, whether their information has already been compromised and is for sale on the dark web, and verify whether their policy documentation is adequate, being followed, and enforced.

> *"He who thinks unknown unknowns and plausible deniability are permanent solutions is the straw that breaks the camel's back."*
> —Ancient InfoSec Proverb

When engaging a third party to assess security status, most organizations start with one or two individual assessments due to limited budgets and resources, rather than an enterprise-wide assessment. Many choose to start with assessments focused on their critical infrastructure, like penetration tests or policy reviews. For example, if your organization relies on a hosted web application, a few third-party cloud environments, and the office network, you may choose to test only those components. This saves a significant amount of capital and is a good way to test the waters with third-party cybersecurity companies. It will also allow for a limited view of the security risk to the organization as opposed to being potentially overwhelmed with an enterprise-wide assessment.

Regardless of whether your initial assessments encompass the entire organization or only specific pieces, be sure that the assessment can answer the following questions:

- **What is our current level of exposure and risk?**
- **Where do the vulnerabilities of concern exist?**
- **What risk is there to our intellectual property and our customers' data?**
- **How can we remediate the vulnerabilities?**
- **In what order should we remediate the vulnerabilities? (Criticality of each).**
- **What is our financial exposure as a result of the current risk? (The likely cost of a breach).**

The security partner that conducts your risk assessments should provide an executive summary with a non-technical overview that everyone can understand. They should also include technical information and evidence of the vulnerabilities, providing actionable information for IT or other technical staff.

Risk assessment documentation should always be tightly controlled and considered highly confidential. After all, it will contain detailed descriptions about where your company is vulnerable and how they can be exploited. Risk assessment documentation should never be provided directly to customers; instead your security partner should provide you with a Letter of Attestation which states your risk level and validates that the testing took place.

Not all cybersecurity companies use the same verbiage. There is often overlap in the terms "risk assessment" and "penetration testing." A risk assessment does not always include penetration testing, and a penetration test does not always include a risk assessment. Further, what some companies are often calling a penetration test, is really no more than an intense scan without any logic, analysis, or attempt to exploit. It is important to ask questions about your security partners' methodology. At Silent Sector, we believe that both, full penetration tests (not just scans) and risk assessments, are necessary, and we typically combine the two, unless specific circumstances dictate otherwise.

Not all penetration tests advertised on the market today are actually penetration tests! Get your penetration tests and cyber risk assessments tailored specifically to your organization. Beware of offers for "one size fits all."

Penetration testing is the process of using the same tools and techniques that a cybercriminal would use to identify and exploit an organization. Silent Sector goes a step beyond most by validating whether a vulnerability is exploitable, rather than simply providing a list of vulnerabilities that may or may not be exploitable, based on your compensating controls. However, penetration tests should stop at demonstrating the capability to exploit a vulnerability, rather than fully exploiting the vulnerability, which may cause unintended consequences such as damage to the environment being tested.

A risk assessment should include a thorough review of the results of a penetration test to define the criticality of each finding and provide recommendations for remediation. As mentioned above, some risk assessments do not include a technical penetration test but accomplish different purposes, such as understanding financial risks or adherence to a compliance framework, i.e., HIPAA, NIST, PCI DSS, or SOC.

3. Define a Path to a Proactive Posture.

An Enterprise Cyber Risk Assessment will present the risks and vulnerabilities that must be remediated based on the risk associated with the findings of the testing. It also provides the starting point for a path to a proactive cybersecurity posture. From there, it is important to act on the findings based on the most critical risk, then set long-term goals to mitigate the remaining identified risks. Additionally, if you have completed a full Business Impact Analysis (BIA) you can leverage those findings to design the proper defense of your company. If you have not completed a BIA, making an internal assessment of your required technologies and their related risks is at the top of your to-do list for establishing proper protection. This should include a plan for future assessments because technologies are constantly changing and new vulnerabilities are identified daily.

During your cyber risk assessment, you'll want to begin considering how your cybersecurity posture will be consistently improved and maintained. Consider how you will address the findings of the assessment with the resources you currently have available. Do you want to leverage in-house professionals to handle the initiative, offload the work to a third-party security partner, or combine both approaches? Your answer will depend on your unique circumstances, internal capabilities, and your budget. We find it most effective to leverage and improve any internal capabilities your organization already has, combined with the support and expertise of your trusted cybersecurity services partner.

4. Build Alliances across Business Units to Facilitate Change.

Whether you hire third-party professionals or add internal staff, it is critical for your IT staff to support new additions to your team. An IT team can sometimes view outside cybersecurity professionals as a threat, due to a fear of outsourcing all aspects of the IT practice. Implementing security introduces a "checks and balances" scenario but all parties should understand that this is for the protection of their organization and it is therefore a benefit to their individual careers. Introduce cybersecurity professionals as extra support for the IT department's efforts, and make it clear they are not there to check up on your existing team's work or poke holes in it.

> *"The Admin who uses 'Admin' all of the time soon becomes the Admin of nothing."*
> —Ancient InfoSec Proverb

While personnel conflicts can occur, most experienced IT professionals welcome the extra support and feel relieved that the security burden does not rest entirely on their shoulders. They are already busy with their keep the lights on (KTLO) work and they'll be especially grateful if they are lacking in experience with a specific framework or requirement. With proper implementation and the right people, cybersecurity and IT professionals will support and learn from each other.

Since cybersecurity affects the company as a whole, it is important to introduce the cybersecurity professionals to other non-technical business units. A good rapport and expectation of potential changes to the environment, process, and new procedures makes the education and awareness process easier throughout the company, and your departments will discover great benefits. For example, the sales team can set itself apart from the competition in prospect meetings by showing it represents an organization with a proactive approach to cybersecurity and is compliant with industry best practices. Further, as security becomes more prevalent, it is becoming standard practice for customers to ask for SOC-2 or other attestations as part of their third-party partner diligence and vendor onboarding. The ability to answer these requests is crucial for software companies, financial services, and anyone that will store or handle confidential data.

5. Have Cybersecurity Professionals Educate Employees and Allow for Participation in Cyber Activities.

Your Clarity and Purpose Statement for cybersecurity should be understood throughout the company. Most people already agree that cybersecurity is important, simply because of the constant breaches they see in the media. However, most users will not truly understand cybersecurity unless they see how it directly impacts their jobs, not just the company as a whole.

Work with Human Resources (HR) to have your cybersecurity professionals implement an organization-wide cybersecurity training program. The program should be designed to increase awareness and help staff members understand how to react when they suspect that something might be malicious.

At a bare minimum, conduct awareness training on an annual basis. Cybersecurity awareness training has become a requirement of most compliance frameworks. We recommend either quarterly or automated ongoing training to maintain a heightened state of awareness.

Your training program can be tailored to different roles within the organization. While all users will experience cyberattacks through phishing (malicious email) or smishing (malicious text message), executives and other high-profile employees will often experience more targeted attacks called "spear phishing." Spear phishing is when a cybercriminal has taken the time to investigate a staff member (executive) and has a knowledge base that allows them to create emails with triggers that will cause them to react. Therefore, training should reflect the threats that leadership and management staff might experience. If your organization is based on a technology product, include more technical training for developers and other engineers to support secure development practices.

6. Identify Your Strengths and Recognize Shortcomings on an Ongoing Basis.

Organizations are in a constant state of change and so is their cyber risk. Your cybersecurity professionals should recommend an appropriate assessment schedule to ensure that you, at a minimum, keep up with the ever-evolving risk environment. The ultimate goal is to keep you at least one step ahead of the cybercriminal.

> *"A cybersecurity program is either growing or dying. There is no pause or stagnation."*
> —Ancient InfoSec Proverb

Most proactive organizations will conduct an annual Enterprise Cyber Risk Assessment. Some perform penetration testing to check for new attack vectors on a biannual or quarterly basis and after significant application or infrastructure changes. Technology-based organizations, such as software companies, may have different frequencies for tests, based on their development lifecycle or other factors. For software developers, it is generally recommended that all code should be scanned for vulnerabilities prior to being promoted to production to ensure that new code doesn't regress any old vulnerabilities or introduce new risk.

The frequency of formal assessment will vary greatly based on the organization. However, vulnerability scanning should be, depending on the size of your enterprise, a daily, weekly, or at minimum, a monthly occurrence. Vulnerability scanning is used to identify risks in your network and web application configurations. Vulnerability scanning can be fully automated. However, a human element is critical to successfully interpret the true risk identified by a scan's output. Silent Sector prefers continuous scanning with a weekly review of the results and immediate review of any significant vulnerabilities that arise.

While vulnerability scanning is an important component of security monitoring, the scan reports are usually not very meaningful to anyone other than the professionals trained to evaluate the results and take appropriate action. Therefore, even automated systems require some human interaction.

7. Staff, Partner, or Outsource to Meet Your Needs.

Always remember that people, not machines, are the foundation of effective security. The next chapter describes the various staffing models for developing and maintaining a cybersecurity program. Regardless of the staffing approach, be sure to identify experienced professionals that you trust, with solid track records, and preferably with advanced cybersecurity credentials from third party governing bodies.

While Silent Sector acknowledges that a certification doesn't necessarily mean someone is qualified to do the job, it will help when searching for the right resource. The cybersecurity industry has made it easy to verify whether someone is a legitimate professional, with recognized certifications. Like many other industries, the cybersecurity industry has multiple authoritative organizations that issue certifications after thorough vetting and testing. These organizations' websites typically have a search function or other methods to easily verify a person's credentials. Some of the major certifying bodies are ISSA, ISC(2), ISACA, EC-Council, PCI, and CompTIA. Both ISACA and ISC(2) require specific amounts of verifiable time in a security position that is attested to by someone who already holds that specific certification, such as the CISSP, CISA, and CRISC.

Due to the practice verification requirements for leadership roles, consider advanced certifications such as CISSP and CRISC, as well as certifications related to any compliance requirements you have, such as PCI-P for PCI DSS compliance.

8. Maintain Documentation.

It is one thing to say that you are being proactive in cybersecurity activities, and another to show it in writing. Every organization needs a complete and current set of documented cybersecurity policies, procedures, and standards tailored to their specific environment. This is also a requirement for most compliance frameworks.

While few IT professionals will admit to enjoying the process of writing a policy document, it is important to document your current policies and processes, then ensure they meet industry standards and compliance requirements. This is especially important when you deal with users who have access to highly confidential data or critical system components. Silent Sector recommends an annual internal audit or even quarterly reviews of your policy, procedure, and standards documents, with updates after major operational changes or changes to your risk posture. All changes should be tracked, including identifying the person who has made the changes. A third-party audit by your cybersecurity partner is recommended annually. This will ensure a fresh set of eyes has reviewed the process to ensure that nothing critical was missed.

> *"I document what I execute and I execute what I document."*
> —Ancient InfoSec Proverb

Cybersecurity documentation includes, at minimum, acceptable use policies, password policies, incident response policies, disaster recovery policies, access and account management, data classification, and other important governance matters.

Documentation should be robust enough to show that the company has put sufficient thought into its protection and incident handling. And the documents must be simple enough that the policies can be implemented without hindering operations.

It is important to not fall into a complacency trap. Many organizations will go through the pain and effort of creating a policy library and then fall back on doing things the way they always have done in the past. This is often seen when extensive change in the day-to-day operations is required.

Many implementations fail by being delayed indefinitely or implemented slowly and soon forgotten. Senior management must sign off, support, and enforce new cybersecurity policies and procedures.

An example from personal experience came while working with a large client in the process of merging with another company. The acquiring company provided policy and procedure documentation to the IT staff of the new company. The policies and procedures were initially followed, but then eventually forgotten.

At the completion of the merger, the acquiring company performed an audit to see if the policies were being followed. It was determined that the new company's IT staff was not following the new policies. They summarily fired the management down to anyone who had power of approval for change. Needless to say, the new policies were taken seriously going forward. Silent Sector never recommends anything that draconian but it is a prime example of unfortunate events that force a change in behavior.

IMPLEMENTATION MODELS

There are a variety of ways to gain support when building a proactive security program. We've listed several options with their pro's and con's below. Ultimately it will come down to what you can afford, the available in-house talent pool, and contractor availability. Regardless of which approach is the best fit, it is absolutely critical that your IT staff, whether in-house or outsourced, understands that adding cybersecurity measures and people is not a risk to their jobs. Leadership must clearly demonstrate the value of their in-house IT professionals and demonstrate that the addition of cybersecurity team members is a benefit to reduce the burden on IT staff while reducing risk for the entire organization. In today's reality, no matter the size of your company, cybersecurity is absolutely critical to your success. Remember, no IT leader wants to be held responsible for a cyber breach, especially if they haven't been allocated the proper resources to defend against it.

DIY MODEL: DO IT YOURSELF

While the "do it yourself" approach is admirable if you are starting a security practice from scratch, it isn't recommended. However, some organizations see it as their only option. It is always great to see brand new companies learning and implementing basic security measures, considering everything else they have on their plate. The DIY approach is far better than doing nothing and if the budget is $0, this is the place to start. Before taking this approach for an emerging or mid-market company, seriously consider everything at risk in the event of a major cyberattack.

PROS	CONS
• DIY is often the only affordable method for startups and small companies. • You'll own and need to configure and maintain any cybersecurity tools and technologies you choose to deploy. • Efforts can grow with the company until another model is accessible.	• DIY is very time-intensive, even if you have experienced IT professionals. • DIY reduces your team's ability to focus on KTLO and growth initiatives. • Unless you hire a senior cybersecurity professional, you will lack guidance coming from proper experience. This leads to confusion and focus on the wrong priorities. • The DIY approach lacks third-party validation of risks or appropriate measures.

HIRE IN-HOUSE CYBERSECURITY PROFESSIONALS

There is simply no replacement for having in-house security professionals who are fully dedicated to the security of your business. This option tends to be out of reach for many companies, due to budget constraints. Those with the ability to build an internal security practice should consider this as a necessity. In today's environment, cybersecurity professionals are in high demand, tough to find, expensive, and hard to keep. Most companies with in-house security professionals augment the internal security program with 3rd party cybersecurity companies for activities that require an outside party, such as cyber risk assessments and penetration tests.

If you are hiring a security professional for the first time, you'll need to find someone with solid experience in building brand-new internal

IMPLEMENTATION MODELS

security practices. It is also an absolute imperative to have buy-in from senior management and all business units. Security touches every aspect of company functions, from HR to Building Maintenance and even the bollards by the front door.

PROS	CONS
• This approach demonstrates a commitment to a mature business model. • In-house staff has a large stake in the game (their reputation and career). • This approach allows for full ownership, leadership, and control over all cyber activities • It generates instant feedback and updates. • It creates an in-house liaison for security or compliance services requiring an outside party.	• It is very expensive because most fully staffed departments require 10+ people. Most companies fail to achieve this number and attempt to run lean. • Partially funded and staffed teams get overburdened and quit. • Assembling the right team for your business is difficult. • There is a high risk of turnover when resources are getting poached by other companies willing to offer more. • One man can't do it all, so you still need a team. • It is tough to find the right people if you don't have in-house expertise to evaluate them.

MANAGED SECURITY SERVICE PROVIDER (MSSP) MODEL

Some organizations choose to outsource as many of the technical aspects of cybersecurity as possible, although an effective cybersecurity program cannot be fully offloaded to a 3rd party. Where the outsourced IT industry has Managed Service Providers (MSPs), the outsourced cybersecurity industry has Managed Security Service Providers, or MSSPs. These companies generally provide a wide spectrum of services that are handled off-site, with a primary focus on security-related tools and products. Unfortunately, many MSSPs serve only large enterprises, pricing themselves out of the market for many small to mid-size businesses. On the bright side, you'll gain access to security professionals and the latest technologies in cyber defense. Even if you outsource most of your technical security requirements, it is still recommended to assign a member of management, or of your KTLO staff, as a security resource to ensure that your priorities are met, rather than receiving a "one size fits all" service from a third party.

PROS	CONS
• Short ramp up time for critical risks and security KTLO. • You quickly have access to multiple types of expertise. • You have more resources available than most companies can afford in-house. • This model can be more cost-effective than building a fully staffed security team in-house. • MSSPs can help smaller companies fill short-term gaps in resources while in-house staff gets up to speed.	• It can be hard to find internal synergy with external entities. Furthermore, a third party isn't going to be as invested in your security as internal resources. • Your company may not always be a MSSPs' first priority, based on expenditure. • Full dependence on an outsourced service can mean significant risk and costs if that service changes, the company fails, or drops the contract.

IMPLEMENTATION MODELS

• MSSPs may include 24/7 monitoring. • MSSPs generally use state-of-the-art technologies.	• MSSPs are sales driven and tend to promote new systems and technologies before maximizing what you already have. • MSSPs often take a "one size fits all" approach. • This approach doesn't empower or place a sense of responsibility on your internal team.

PARTNERED SECURITY SERVICE PROVIDER™ (PSSP) MODEL

The Partnered Security Services Provider™ (PSSP) model provides outside support that integrates with any IT and/or security staff that you might already have. You can consider this a co-managed security department or extended security team. The addition of cybersecurity expertise allows you to leverage and empower your current internal resources.

This is Silent Sector's preferred approach for most organizations, because it allows the development of a proper security posture both internally and externally. In other words, a partnered model allows you to maximize any internal capabilities and technologies, before investing in new systems or people. This model also helps your current IT professionals and other staff build their capabilities, while providing the support necessary for their priorities to remain focused on core initiatives.

PROS	CONS
• Maximize the results with the investments you've already made in technology, processes, and people. • Resolve cybersecurity deficits quickly. • Bring in high-level skill sets at a fraction of the cost of hiring in-house staff. • Build effective security from the inside to reduce full reliance on third parties. • Maintain agility to meet customer needs, while meeting compliance requirements and adding manpower. • Create an opportunity for on-the-job training for existing staff. • PSSP can support implementation as well as advice.	• PSSP is not the same as staff augmentation for your in-house IT and/or security team. Their hours are limited to a fraction of a week. • A PSSP spends time with multiple clients and therefore cannot support as many; making them harder to come by. • Providers can sometimes be expensive and use a variety of names for this approach. The level of expertise also varies. • Some compliance requirements, such as a SOC 2, may need to be conducted by a truly independent party, not the partner assisting in your KTLO cybersecurity matters. • Some PSSPs function as advisors only, so ensure you have the appropriate implementation support you need.

WILL AN IT COMPANY COVER OUR CYBERSECURITY?

"Cybersecurity" has become a buzzword and companies are jumping on the bandwagon, trying to get a piece of that market. The marketplace is flooded with companies saying that they handle cybersecurity. Some really are equipped to build a cybersecurity program and provide adequate services, while many are being very misleading. Sure, all companies' advertising cybersecurity may offer something that has to

IMPLEMENTATION MODELS

do with the subject, but most are only handling a fraction of the big picture. It is important to understand the difference between an IT company or managed service provider (MSP), and a company that has the ability to build and maintain a holistic cyber risk management program.

The majority of players in this industry are focused on selling technology products and tools, as discussed throughout this book. IT companies or MSPs will generally sell and manage infrastructure and cloud solutions that have a security component. After all, cybersecurity works on a defense-in-depth model, touching everything in an organization's environment. Therefore, if a MSP claims, *"We offer cybersecurity"* when what they really do is set up firewalls and other infrastructure, they are not being transparent and telling the whole story. In this case, they provide one component of cybersecurity but what about the strategy, assessments, testing, governance, training, compliance, and myriads of other considerations that go into a proper cybersecurity program? A MSP will generally install appliances and provide remote monitoring services, only a small slice of the cybersecurity pie.

It is important to understand who is doing what to protect your organization from cyber criminals. You must have a primary, internal or external, professional overseeing all the various factors, vendors, and requirements, in order to be effective at cyber risk management.

For a deeper dive into the topic of MSPs and IT companies providing cybersecurity, visit the later chapter, "Where do MSPs Fit in a Cybersecurity Program?"

CYBERSECURITY EXPENDITURES

Do not be fooled by the many commoditized cybersecurity service offerings which are promising protection for a small monthly fee that is the same for everyone. Choosing a cheap, one size fits all, cyber risk management service ends up being far more expensive than a solution customized to your organization.

The cost of cybersecurity depends on a wide variety of variables, including company size, data retention requirements, reliance on technology, where the technology lives, and what type of systems are used. The following figures represent Silent Sector's best efforts to provide an approximate range for common services and implementations staff salaries. Your solution might consist of multiple components, so actual costs will vary accordingly.

Below is a list of average salaries for Security professionals in the Phoenix, AZ area (per Salary.com), at the time of this writing. Salaries will vary by location.

In-House Staff Salaries*:

- CISO (Chief Information Security Officer): $225,131 per year.
- Senior Security Analyst: $89,632 per year.
- Security Manager: $92,982 per year.

*Based on Salary.com figures in Phoenix, AZ as of 2020.

This service pricing is based on industry knowledge, research, and quotations from various providers. Again, figures vary greatly based on the size of the organization, complexity, industry and compliance requirements, in-house capabilities, and more factors. Cybersecurity services firms will engage in a thorough discussion about scoping, usually under NDA, to develop appropriate plans and proposals at either fixed project or hourly rates.

Outsourced/MSSP Model:

- Small-midsize companies: $10,000—$25,000 per month.
- Large organizations: $25,000—$100,000+ per month.

Partnership/Team Augmentation Model (PSSP):

- $50,000—$250,000 per year.

SPECIFIC SERVICES

Enterprise Cyber Risk Assessment:
- Small organization: $25,000—$50,000
- Large enterprise: $50,000—$250,000

Web Application Penetration Testing:
- Small application: $8,500—$25,000
- Large application: $25,000—$80,000

Network Penetration Testing:
- Small environment: $10,000—$40,000
- Large environment: $40,000—$150,000

Qualified & Experienced Consulting:
- $275—$400 per hour, as needed or in predefined blocks (e.g. 20 hours). Rates may be reduced for long-term engagements (as hourly requirements increase).

IMPLEMENTATION TIPS

Regardless of which model or combination of models might be right for your organization, be sure to work with trustworthy and experienced professionals with proper credentials. Ask about their strengths and weaknesses, and take your time getting to know them. Choose people you'll enjoy working with, especially if they'll be integrated with your team. Be sure to work with professionals who can explain highly technical subjects in a simplified manner that everyone can understand.

Your cybersecurity partner probably isn't the right fit if you find they are more interested in your dollars than results, with the next five billable projects lined up, none of which mesh with your needs.

> *"Strong cybersecurity knowledge does not discriminate, it serves many industries and types of companies."*
> —Ancient Infosec Proverb

Cybersecurity professionals don't necessarily need a background in your specific industry. The same technologies are used across many different organizations around the world, making strong cybersecurity experience far more important selection criteria than industry involvement. Even the various compliance frameworks, such as NIST, PCI-DSS, SOC, and HIPAA, have many similarities. Understanding how to navigate cybersecurity compliance and audits is more essential than a specific framework. Sure, some industries such as healthcare and manufacturing have unique technologies, but the fundamentals of security remain the same.

Knowing these facts will open more options in the talent pool. When you take a deep dive into each security framework and compliance requirements, you'll start to see that the basic principles are the same. There is a tremendous amount of overlap and many of the same points are simply stated differently between documents.

HOW TO ENSURE ONGOING PROTECTION

Security programs only succeed with top-down support. An effective program requires backing from leadership at the highest levels, due to the potential enterprise-wide impact, changes, and financial liability within an enterprise.

In the event of a breach, reactive security is a major financial expense resulting in diminished brand credibility, lost clientele, and a major delay in operations. Therefore, leadership must be willing to allocate resources and funding to proactive security, or at minimum, a plan to combine the proactive and reactive security. The least desirable alternative is to set aside a significant level of resources for reactive measures, in anticipation of a breach.

IMPLEMENTATION MODELS

Leadership must be present to mediate issues and challenges that arise between business units and the cybersecurity team. Leadership and cybersecurity management must work together to overcome common misconceptions, such as the common belief that security will negatively affect production or cos t more than it is worth.

There is a good reason you'll hear us rant over and over, "Security starts with leadership." Stated another way, without leadership support, cyber risk runs rampant.

Continuous cybersecurity oversight is especially critical for companies that do not currently have compliance requirements, simply because there is no outside governance forcing security initiatives. This situation is becoming a rare occurrence and should follow that trend, especially considering there are proposed legislations in Congress to force security requirements on all companies. Regardless of your specific requirements, always remember that cybersecurity is not a one-time activity. At a minimum, you'll need annual assessment, testing, and improvements to maintain an appropriate level of protection.

EXPERTISE-DRIVEN CYBERSECURITY®

expert —*noun*—ˈek-ˌspərt: one with the special skill or knowledge representing mastery of a particular subject. (Source: Merriam-Webster)

The word "expert" has different meanings to different people. From "script kiddies" to advanced persistent threat (APT) actors, expertise is relative in cybersecurity and tends to be in the "eye of the beholder." Experts are everywhere. It is important to understand how to find and leverage the appropriate types of expertise in order to achieve your business objectives. In this chapter, we will explore how security professionals should be positioned, what factors make an effective cybersecurity expert, and why expertise is more important than technology.

WHAT THE CYBERSECURITY INDUSTRY CAN LEARN FROM ASYMMETRICAL WARFARE

In many ways, the fight against cybercrime can be compared to the Global War on Terror. Often, the two go hand-in-hand as many cyber criminals are funding terrorist operations. While cyber-attacks take a different, less bloody approach when compared to terrorist attacks, the threat actors function in a similar manner.

Much like modern terrorist networks, cybercrime rings tend to operate with criminals spread around the world. They are decentralized organizations lacking a clear hierarchical structure. Cybercrime rings are usually comprised of individuals who are dedicated to specific areas of expertise or have access to certain assets of interest. They primarily strike "soft targets" which are those that offer the highest gain or impact relative to the amount of risk and resource expenditure. In cybercrime, these targets are generally the organizations with the least cybersecurity protection or with poorly implemented security measures.

Why is this comparison between terrorist organizations and cybercrime rings important? The U.S. Army and other military organizations around the world have completely transformed the way they look at warfare in today's dynamic environment. It is no longer only the massive forces of other countries that we are concerned about. To combat today's threats, our military has learned to run leaner, more nimble units with a major emphasis on intelligence.

Expertise is now the most critical asset of special operations units designed to protect the Nation against terrorist attacks. We believe expertise is also the most important asset for organizations in the fight against cybercrime. It takes strong expertise to plan, organize, execute, and learn from operations, both in counterterrorism and on the cybersecurity front.

The approach of special operations units, leveraging expertise and operating at high levels of autonomy with smaller, more nimble forces, has proven tremendously effective in the War on Terror. This approach is credited for saving countless numbers of lives. Why is it that the cybersecurity industry is still focused on building conglomerates and hierarchical structures instead of nimble organizations with high levels of autonomy and expertise, providing the "boots on the ground" support to protect companies from cyber-attacks? It has become all about financial status and shareholder gain... That's why.

THE ELEMENTS OF EXPERTISE

Expertise is the foundational component of an effective cybersecurity program. Considering the vast number of disciplines in the cybersecurity industry, nobody can be an expert in all areas. It is critical to find the right mix of security professionals who possess the combination of expertise that will be the most beneficial to your organization's specific needs. For example, a world-renowned mobile application penetration tester may be great to test the security of your mobile application but would not be the right fit if what your company really needs is to build a security program that aligns with an industry standard framework.

Experts with experience across multiple types of organizations and industries tend to be best suited to guide and support mid-market companies in developing a proactive security posture. These experts have dealt with a range of security and compliance issues over multiple years and have relationships with other experts able to cover niche requirements and disciplines. Most think of expertise as being a factor of experience, education, and credentials. We believe other key factors must be present in order for one individual to truly be considered an expert.

A true expert must have exceptional knowledge and hands-on experience, coupled with a good attitude and a strong mindset in order to produce the highest level of performance. Attitude is the single most important factor determining success or failure in any project or organization. Many studies have shown that a positive attitude produces a higher level of creativity, enhanced memory, and more efficient engagement of the brain's problem-solving capacity. A strong mindset allows a security expert to continuously learn and improve. It allows one to be comfortable with the fact that many solutions will be difficult to obtain and work well in a team environment, seeking support from other experts as needed.

When you are seeking the support of an expert in any field, always think beyond the resume.

PEOPLE > TECHNOLOGY

People are more important than tools and technology. In today's environment, where a shortage of security professionals is a common issue, an overwhelming emphasis is being placed on cybersecurity tools and technologies. Most companies claiming to be "cybersecurity service providers" are focused almost primarily on reselling security products.

However, cybersecurity professionals understand that tools and technology alone will not stop cyber criminals. Of course, tools and technology are a necessity. The industry must continue to innovate and create solutions for the work humans cannot possibly do in a timely manner. Still, dedicated expertise and the human element is the most effective weapon in the fight against cybercrime.

Luckily, the cybersecurity industry has developed several training programs and certifying bodies, allowing one to quickly understand the areas of focus and the specific skill sets of cyber professionals. Organizations such as ISSA, ISACA, ISC(2), EC-Council, and others have developed certifications for all levels, from novice to seasoned professional. Certifications such as CISSP, CRISC, CEH-Practical, and OSCP have specific, industry recognized criteria and strict testing standards. While the focus of this chapter is not about the specific certifications, it is important to recognize that these credentials are out there and provide a helpful first step to validate capabilities when vetting cybersecurity staff or partners.

It is also important to understand that all tools and technologies available are only designed to support a very small segments of an organization's security posture. Expert practitioners think beyond the technology. They evaluate and improve security programs with a holistic point of view, not only based on current trends, but also drawing from years of experience. Technologies alone will always fail to protect the companies relying on them if they fail to leverage a proper strategy and expert implementation.

CASE STUDY: GROWING SAAS COMPANY WITH ENTERPRISE PROSPECTS

Silent Sector was engaged by "SimTechx" (fictitious name for confidentiality purposes and not related to any company named "SimTechx" if one actually exists), a SaaS company selling an enterprise platform. SimTechx has over 300 employees, including many developers, and is well funded by venture capital. As the company grew, it sought large enterprise contracts and ran headfirst into a serious roadblock.

SimTechx's cloud-based software is relied upon by companies across a variety of industries. As a result, the company eventually found that it was being held to stringent security standards and was required to align with multiple compliance frameworks. As it turns out, SimTechx was not meeting those requirements.

The company's security posture was nowhere near the strength that the company assumed internally. It took lost prospects and revenue opportunities for SimTechx to realize that something different needed to be done. Prior to leveraging human expertise, the company measured its security posture using a series of off-the-shelf compliance and risk management tools for a hefty monthly fee. These tools had beautiful user interfaces and produced simple, one-page reports on demand. These reports stated that the company was in compliance with its requirements, secure, and all was well... Until it wasn't. Tens of thousands of dollars were spent for inaccurate and incomplete, auto-generated reports from these so-called "cybersecurity" platforms.

Early in the onboarding process, Silent Sector's team saw the roots of the issues and pointed out the security flaws, inaccurate reports, and cyber risk exposure, while developing a roadmap to achieve the level of security required by enterprise clients.

It turns out that what SimTechx really needed was expertise from cybersecurity professionals, not more tools and dashboards. Silent Sector's team provided guidance and support for the developers, IT staff, and corporate leadership, that automation simply could not

CYBER RANTS

handle. With this new expertise in hand, SimTechx was able to dispose of the unnecessary tools, reduce costs, create clarity, and regain the trust of enterprise prospects.

With leadership commitment and a systematic approach, cybersecurity experts can guide you to maximize the security posture of your organization without major technology expenditures. When new tools are required, expert cybersecurity professionals take an unbiased, technology agnostic approach, and make recommendations based on needs rather than product margins and commissions.

If you feel you're lacking tools or technology, first seek ways to accomplish your objectives with what you already have by seeking professional guidance. If it is determined that a new technology solution is needed, seek an unbiased, brand agnostic, comparative analysis of the various tools that might meet your requirements.

Silent Sector's Expertise-Driven Cybersecurity® approach is built on our industry and technology expertise, combined with tactics and strategies used by the U.S. Special Forces. By leveraging this experience and knowledge, companies are able to achieve impactful and verifiable results. They are strengthening their security posture while using less time and fewer resources.

We believe that leveraging the expertise and dedicated focus of security professionals is the only effective approach to protect mid-market and emerging companies from cyber-attacks.

BUILDING AND KEEPING THE TEAM

If your organization struggles to find and retain talent, don't worry, you're not alone. In fact, a common question we get from many clients is, *"How do we find and keep good IT people, especially security people, in this competitive hiring environment?"* This chapter will show you how to build and retain top talent. And yes, there is a lot more to consider than simply offering larger salaries.

The Issue

As of this writing, there are far more open IT jobs than there are qualified IT professionals to fill them. This has created a seller's market, putting the job market in the hands of the professionals, not the employers. Regardless of the market or economy, most IT and security teams are running very lean. Teams that are not part of KTLO operations often run leaner than the rest of the IT organization. Simultaneously, security threats are increasing exponentially in quantity and complexity, while qualified IT and security staff available to handle them are scarce. By the year 2021, it is estimated that there will be 3.5 million unfilled cybersecurity positions. The cost of cybercrime is estimated to reach nearly 6 trillion dollars annually, which includes the cost to restore and mitigate damage. Ransomware attacks occur approximately every 11 seconds, causing over 20 billion dollars a year in economic loss. What is often overlooked is the recovery cost from a ransomware attack. The cost to fully recover is often substantially larger than the actual ransom paid to the cybercriminal.

CYBER RANTS

Key numbers that should concern everyone: 85% of all companies do not have sufficient cybersecurity staff; there will be an estimated 3.5 million unfilled positions in 2021; there is a ransomware attack every 11 seconds, and the cybercrime industry is estimated to be worth 6 trillion dollars per year. Cybercriminals will not stop their attacks, as illustrated by these numbers! They will also continue to take full advantage of turmoil, like the COVID-19 pandemic.

To add to the complexity of finding and keeping qualified cybersecurity resources, there are multiple stages in an IT person's career, each with different interests for their next career move. Due to the shortage of qualified IT and security professionals, job openings are often posted in a broad format to attract the largest number of candidates possible. Instead, job ads should be tailored specifically to the resource you are trying to recruit, at the right stage of their career.

For example, a great employee who fits your needs at the beginning stage of their career may not stick around unless their job changes as they transition to the next stage of their career. It is important to determine whether your organization has a career transition plan in place or if it is just filling the needs of the moment.

A mid-career employee may be an ideal fit for an entry-level position, at least temporarily, and may even take the job out of necessity. However, they often grow bored quickly and look for other positions as options present themselves.

Senior-level resources who are highly qualified for any position you may have are looking for better quality of life and benefits, like working from home, work-life balance, new technologies, and opportunities for upward mobility, while being less concerned about money or stock options. Depending on what your organization is able to offer, the most qualified candidate for your open position may not be the best candidate for the job.

For a variety of circumstances, IT staff tend to change jobs, on average, every 18 months in a good economy. However, they are less likely to leave their current geographic location, especially if they are more advanced in their career. As IT management changes and technologies evolve, companies often create their own problems, which cause them to lose good employees. For example, an experienced Cisco or Microsoft resource may not be a great F5 or Linux resource. They may not even have an interest in learning the new technologies, depending on what career stage they are in.

We constantly get asked the question, *"How do I find and retain good security resources?"* To answer this, we started by thinking about why we took on or changed jobs over the years coupled with what we are seeing today. We thought we'd take a trip through a few of our early career gigs to find the common threads. Into bat country we go!

How Do You Find Good Cybersecurity Professionals?

Be mindful of the fact technologists were technical before they ever had a job. Continuing to feed that desire for understanding, learning, and knowledge will go a long way to ensuring an employee is retained or hired, as long as they are well compensated and treated with respect. This is especially relevant at the beginning of the professional's career.

Technologists have different wants and needs through the various stages of their careers but we will focus on the common threads. Work life balance may not mean anything to a single 20-something year old but it can be everything to a 30 or 40 years old who is married with 2 young kids.

We'll divide the IT career into 4 stages: Newbie, Beginner, Mid-level, and Senior. These are chronological stages for the purpose of this writing and not necessarily based on knowledge. However, there is a corollary between the two. In this section, co-author Mike Rotondo, will share his career choices at each phase to illustrate the progression.

CYBER RANTS

> *"When one is eager to learn, no obstacle or task is too mundane or challenging to overcome, even PCI compliance."*
> —Ancient Infosec Proverb

Newbie:

As a newly minted Microsoft Certified Solutions Expert (MCSE), my first real IT gig was for a hotel chain, working and travelling to run cable, install and patch servers, install MS Office, and general onsite helpdesk, plus some Y2K preparation work thrown in for good measure. The reason I took this job was for the opportunity to get some experience on my resume, make some money, have a challenge, and travel.

Beginner:

We were in the dotcom era after my contract IT gig ended. I found my next job working at a promising dotcom. My interview consisted of some basic technical questions and proof of my MCSE. I was hired on the spot contingent on one test...

They handed me a stack of Windows NT 4.0 floppy discs and a stack Lotus Notes floppy disks. I was told that I had 3 days to build a mail server. Mission accomplished!

I spent the next 4 years on the leading edge of technology. I could build and troubleshoot a server in my sleep, worked 16 to 18-hour days, slept in my office, worked in a downtown high-rise that had a game room with ping pong and a pool table, stocked kitchen, and power beers. I could have margaritas every day at 4:00 and pretty much all the pizza I could eat.

Why does IT management believe that if you buy me pizza, I will work myself to death? Do they think I can't get my own pizza and eat it at home? But I digress. The largest draw for this job was being on the leading edge of technology and the "new" economy. Also, and I can't stress this enough, the stock options promised my efforts would directly impact my financial future. So, the motivation for staying there was the challenge. I had a bit of pride in building the "new future," gaining experience, getting trained on new technology, and money, of course, but not pizza.

Needless to say, after the dotcom bust my stock options weren't worth a slice of pizza. I took this job to add to my resume and to challenge and expand my skill set. The stock options and Internet billionaires riding around in their Ferraris were always in the back of my mind, but it wasn't about the money.

Mid-Level:

My next opportunity was with a company that was not local, not regional, but national… For me, at this stage, it was the big times with a big pay day! It got me travelling with the corporate card to exciting places like New York, LA, San Francisco, Seattle, Las Vegas, Atlanta… and as a bonus, Cleveland, Des Moines, and Pittsburgh. I loved the job, when I started. I enjoyed the tech, my team, the pay and bonuses, based on my performance and when I extended engagements. Eventually, I was forced to take more of a management role and spend more time in meetings than with technology. This meant that I had to hire, fire, and deal with HR issues. It got to a point where I knew airport gate agents by name at multiple airports. I could tell you a hotel chain by looking at a fabric swatch and regularly slept in airports due to missed or cancelled flights. That's when I knew it was time for something else.

> *"It's not that you can't teach an old IT person new tricks, sometimes an IT person is happy with the tricks they know."*
> —Ancient Infosec Proverb

Senior Positions:

Before starting Silent Sector, I had moved to in-house roles and my last several jobs were quite often lateral moves with large companies. I made more money, had the opportunity to work from home, with little to no travel. As I aged, benefits and 401(k)s began to matter more. I was less willing to entertain the idea of equity trades for work. The one thing I enjoyed most was having the ability to be a technology influencer and decision maker. The work from home and quality of life meant more than other aspects of the job as I moved forward in my career. However, the continual politics and poor decisions being made by some of the management always caused me to move on.

WHAT DOES AN IDEAL IT EMPLOYEE WANT?

You may have noticed common threads running through the phased story above. In fact, the only true difference in many of the career move factors is the weight each person applies to the decision of whether to take a position with Company A or Company B. You may have noticed that compensation wasn't even a factor in the decision to take on the first position. So, do you know what your IT resources really want?

1. Compensation is important but not always the most important factor. Keep in mind that most technical people were technical long before they were employed. Do not, however, discount the weight of this factor. Lower pay for being able to play with the latest and greatest tech may be okay for some people but after the first year or two, it no longer matters to most.

2. Good working environment—Remember, there are sites like Glassdoor and LinkedIn that will give your prospective employee a window into your company and its working environment.

3. Taking into account compensation—You have to look at the environment in which your resources will work: Okay Pay + Bad

Environment = Unhappy Employees. However, Great Environment + Okay Pay = Happy Employees. This is just an oversimplification of the fact that a great working environment may make up for lower pay, but it has to be what your employees consider great, not necessarily what management thinks is great. *"Free pizza anyone?"*

4. Politics or the lack thereof? This ties into the environment in which the resource will work. A friend who has spent years as a corporate trainer shared that, based on his years of analysis, technical people in general have little to no tolerance for palace intrigue or company politics. We fully concur with this statement. Another interesting point from this friend is that technologists are far more offended when you speak negatively of their work than when you speak negatively of them as a person.

5. Respect. Not just respect from peers, but also from other departments, especially leadership—To get the best work out of an IT resource, they need to be supported in their decisions by management, as well as by senior management. The security team needs to be able to speak the truth about risks in the environment without fear of retribution.

6. Exposure to new technologies—The internal dialogue of an employee might sound like this: "Am I on the bleeding or at least cutting edge, or is this company a late adopter? What does it mean for my resume if I am 3 years behind everyone else?"

7. Training—Is the company investing in training and building skillset as well as supporting certification requirements, like CPE (Continuing Professional Education)?

8. Travel—This will be subjective to the individual, but travel often becomes more of a negative as a career advances (although that

will depend on the amount of travel). Everyone loves the occasional trip or out of state conference to mix things up a bit.

9. The ability to impact the technical direction of the company creates a strong sense of meaning and significance in the job.
10. Stability in the job becomes more important towards mid-to-senior career.
11. Opportunity for advancement and job growth become less important after mid-career.
12. Work-life balance becomes more important as the professional's career advances. Work from home opportunities should be extended to your senior employees. Work from home rights are earned based on experience on the job, not necessarily something to be given freely to newbies. This approach gives the new employees something to work towards.

Soap Box Moment

Security and technical resources must be treated respectfully by all departments. We can't tell you how many meetings we have attended where an application, hardware, or security SME is shouted down or treated poorly by employees (especially management or PMs) outside their reporting structure. All too often, managers are silently allowing their employees to take on the abuse. Your technical resources are the experts on your technology and security teams and should be treated as such. These employees know what is right, from a technical perspective, and they have very valid reasons for asking the "hard" questions, for saying "no," or for insisting on specific requirements for new software. They know far better than non-technical resources, even if those have such titles as "Director," "Manager," or "VP."

THE SEARCH

There are standard recruitment lines you can find in any Internet search. We have found 372,000 in .55 seconds using Google. They are full of simplistic statements, such as *"build retention policies and improve your hiring process," "find the right team member match," "show your employees the future," "make sure employees fit your culture," "make sure employees are passionate about your company,"* but what exactly does any of that mean? Arguably those simple statements are subjective to the individual employee and industry.

To be transparent, I was never passionate about the companies I worked for in the past. I was passionate about my work and my paycheck clearing but rarely the company itself, until starting Silent Sector. I was not alone. This is common with IT and security staff in large organizations.

We have found and happen to agree with Entrepreneur.com about 3 points describing the type of employee you are looking for: (comments added are ours).

1. They want more—They are not satisfied doing the minimum and are not looking to just skate by, they want to be successful.

2. They're weird—Let the freak flag fly and let's be creative! This creativity, believe it or not, is especially critical in security and software development.

3. They like to prove others wrong—That generally means they are creative, confident, and have an ego, so they will figure out a way to make their ideas successful. The downside of this is unless you keep this person challenged and they know their input is heard and respected, they will quickly move on to another company or will simply revert to do the minimum, miserably, until they can find another gig. One caveat on this. It can also be negative and disruptive if they do not have the talent to back up this attitude and if it is not managed properly.

Aptitude testing is a common topic found in the recruiting "how to" web pages. Ask yourself, *"Is aptitude testing the solution to finding a good employee?"* Not everyone responds well to standard tests. A better measure may be a certification, like a CISSP, CRISC, or CISA, which requires verification of their work. In short, proof that they can do the job. ISC2 and ISACA have already figured out if they are qualified to do the work. For developers, there are simple code checks to confirm that they know the basics or problem-solving questions. Just don't ask, *"If you were a tree, what kind of a tree would you be?"*

Everyone has an opinion but not everyone's opinion should carry the same weight when determining your options.

Another common thread is to check out the prospective employees' social media accounts. We personally find that a little creepy and invasive. How would you feel if they checked out yours? That being said, there is one caveat on social media; reviewing accounts as part of the interview/hiring process. A prospective employee that engages actively in social media and posts extensive personal information is a ripe target for social engineering attacks and could potentially be a weak link in your security team. When you check out the social media presence of a potential employee, look beyond the posts where they are doing a keg stand at the lake. Look at what they are posting and their biography. Is their name, address, phone number, parents' and kids' names, pets' names, birthdays, etc., posted on Facebook, Twitter, or Instagram? If so, that could indicate someone who might not understand how to protect their information. If they are not concerned enough to protect their own Personally Identifiable Information (PII) or their Highly Confidential (HC) data, are they going to protect yours?

BUILDING AND KEEPING THE TEAM

Looking at a prospective employee's social media is still creepy and invasive. We're not saying, "don't do it." Just don't talk about it in public.

Generalities, but Not One Size Fits All!

1. Define the career stage of the resource you are seeking. This will allow you to refine your search and target people at the ideal point in their career.

2. Narrowly defined job postings will at least get qualified applicants' attention. If your request for someone who knows PERL, Splunk, Metasploit, Sophos, Palo Alto, Windows Server and is a PCI or SOX expert, you may get applicants but not necessarily the best since the person with all these requirements probably doesn't exist. If they do, their knowledge is probably too shallow in those areas to be a true expert. Be specific about what you are looking for in an employee.

3. Networking—get out of the office and go to an ISACA, ISSA, or ISC2 meeting. You can pick one of the literally 100s of IT groups on Meetup.com. Observe and engage the attendees and you might make a connection. Ask for referrals from the good people you meet that might not fit your requirements.

4. In your ad, call out that you will PROVIDE TRAINING—This is all caps for a reason. If you cannot afford training, at the very least, allow your team to get their continuing professional education (CPE) and pay them for their time out of the office, including out of state conferences, like Black Hat, RSA, or Defcon. If you want resources with security certifications, be aware that there are CPE requirements annually to maintain those certifications. Support your employees and protect your company by allowing them time to obtain CPE. Please keep in mind that security is not static; it

continually changes. This is why it is an absolute imperative that your security staff remain current on trends, technologies, risks, and new security techniques.

If IT and security professionals don't stay current, they become obsolete and the organization they work for becomes obsolete. Always support your team in continuing to learn, innovate, and improve!

5. People are less willing to relocate out of state or even commute long distances for a new position. Consider remote work when you can't find a resource in your city. Smaller cities like Milwaukee, Pittsburgh, Cleveland, Tucson, Mobile, and Cheyenne may not have the depth and quality of resources needed and someone from LA, San Francisco, Phoenix, or Chicago may not want to move there. In fact, with the shortage of qualified security staff nationwide, larger cities don't have all the talent they need either.

6. Look at what your competitors are offering and do better. For example, an extra 3 to 5 sick or vacation days go a long way and will cost less than having team members who lack qualifications.

7. Advertise the best qualities of your company, sick/vacation days, flex schedule, 401(k) matching, along with a list of quality restaurants, bars, and housing close to the office, etc.

8. In this economy, you must sell your company to prospective employees, especially if you can't beat the competition with compensation.

9. Promote the vision by describing the successful person in the role, not just the job applicant's traits.

10. Get referrals from your current staff. Ask your team first when a new position opens. If they don't know anyone, there might be another issue to address with your corporate culture.

> *"A true geek was a geek before being paid to be one."*
> —Ancient Infosec Proverb

COMPENSATION: SHOW ME THE MONEY!!!

We need to address the elephant in the room, compensation. There is no way around it and most employers are not going to like it, but we must reiterate the following statistics: By the year 2021 (that's next year as of this writing), it is predicted that there will be 3.5 million unfilled cybersecurity positions and the cost of cybercrime is estimated to be nearly 6 trillion dollars annually.

Corporations are going to have to revise their thinking when it comes to compensation for IT security resources. One way to start is to decouple the corporate pay structure from IT KTLO staff. You may be thinking that this doesn't sound fair or *"that sounds right and I understand where you are coming from."* In this job market, you must remember that security engineers are specialized, and quality security engineers are becoming rare. Further, we need to dispel the notion that you can train anyone to be a good or even an adequate cybersecurity engineer, much less a great one. You can't do it, any more than you can train anyone off the street to be a great developer. We have no statistics or science to back that statement up, just our experience which goes back several decades. We can tell you, based on our observations, that not all IT people are talented or created equal. There are alphas, betas, and then the drones (people who are comfortable doing the same work for decades). You need the Alphas and Betas to succeed as an organization. Drones do serve a purpose, but an army of drones only gets you so far.

> *"Money can't buy you love and devotion but it can rent it 40 hours a week."*
> —Ancient Infosec Proverb

The stratified job families and pay structures may have worked in the past. However, with the resource shortage and other criteria that will come into play later, good technical professionals are going to go toward the money and career-building opportunities. That place will most likely be consulting, which means that instead of paying $130 an hour for a fully burdened resource, with benefits and other overhead, companies will be paying $350 or more per hour for a "mercenary" consulting firm.

Companies working to keep talent in-house must develop specific job categories for security engineers that are not tied to their current job classification of "Infrastructure Engineer 1–5" or similar definitions. Instead, develop "security job families" and pay them at a higher rate. It simply comes down to supply and demand. Right now, the supply is low and there is a huge demand, which continues to increase. The growing demand can be additionally evidenced with initiatives by the Federal Government. Congress began to discuss a data privacy policy similar to GDPR and it is considering holding executives (decision makers) criminally liable, as in jail time, for breeches. Also, the Cybersecurity Maturation Model Certification (CMMC) requirements will be enforced for all defense contractors, not just the Tier 1 companies.

Below are examples of IT KTLO salaries and IT security salaries listed on Payscale.com at the time of this writing. There are similar tables at Indeed, Zip Recruiter, and other sites. We have matched them up, based on expected experience and responsibilities. There are some geographic areas that will pay more because the standard cost of living is much higher, for example New York City versus Mobile. If you look at the numbers on those sites, you can see IT salaries range anywhere

BUILDING AND KEEPING THE TEAM

from $36,000—$324,000 in the U.S., depending on geography and job classification.

- Average Information Security Analyst Salary: $70,397
- Average Systems Engineer (Computer Networking/IT): $72,365
- Average Information Security Specialist: $75,263
- Average Database Administrator (DBA) Salary: $71,929
- Average Microsoft Exchange Administrator Salary: $73,906
- Average Security Architect, IT Salary: $121,031
- Average Solutions Architect Salary: $115,824

Based on the figures above, the difference in pay is insignificant between KTLO and security resources until they reach the architect level. At that level, the difference in pay is based on the amount of training and experience required to become a security architect, the scarcity of the qualified architects, and the potential impact to the company if security is not staffed with quality resources. While we would be fools to argue that there isn't also a shortage of good KTLO IT resources, the supply is arguably lower for qualified and experienced cybersecurity resources. In reality, we would be happy to see all IT salaries rise considering the hours that IT professionals work and the sacrifices of time that are expected but that is another conversation altogether.

> *"A skilled cyber warrior is an investment for the wise. The higher the skill of the warrior, the higher the cost of the services and the better the results on the battlefield."*
> —Ancient InfoSec Proverb

The argument can be made, and we have made it, that without the underlying infrastructure, the security resource is irrelevant. We could also argue that without the billing and accounting teams, the marketing team, or the sales team, the infrastructure is irrelevant. In short, while you cannot fully remove one team from a company without impacting the whole organization, the security team ensures that all the work done by the other teams is protected and safe for customer use. And this allows the company to be profitable and maintain a positive brand image in the long run.

Cybersecurity resources need to be categorized in a different way than other IT resources and paid differently. Corporate investment in training and CPE of their resources should be mandatory. This would ensure that they remain relevant and up to date with this rapidly changing field to safeguard the security, brand integrity, and profitability of the enterprise. There are multiple factors that impact a resource's decision to either take or stay at a position but it would be foolish to deny that income may have a larger impact in the decision-making process than many other factors, excluding perhaps geography and relocation. We reveal the unwillingness of many resources to relocate, especially to cities with a high cost of living, like New York, LA, San Francisco, or Seattle. This is a justifiable argument for the expansion of remote work but more on that later.

THE PROCESS

"OK genius, you told me what they want, why I have to pay them more, and how to attract them. So, after I do all that, how do I keep them?"

Qualified security and IT resources are scarce, and the demand is continuing to escalate, thereby creating valid questions, such as *"how do I retain them once they're hired?"* We'll give you the secret when we find it but for now, there is no magic formula. IT resources all have different factors driving their decision-making process in regards to their career choices. Some stay in jobs because they don't know if there is anything better out there for them. Some "drones" are happy performing the same tasks for 35 years and then retiring. While you need drones for basic functions, what you really want are rock stars

BUILDING AND KEEPING THE TEAM

(Alphas) to lead your IT and security teams. You have to get creative to find and keep Alphas.

The traditional work model in corporate America, the one that has been around since... well... forever, may work for certain divisions in your company, but it will not continue to work for IT. While engineers and musicians have much in common, IT resources can be compared to artists. Good IT resources are highly intelligent, inquisitive, and creative. They consume more information in a day than most people do in a month. Most of them work best in small groups of two or three task-oriented people, or alone.

IT and security professionals are certainly different from your other resources. If you don't believe me, think about this the next time you walk through the IT section of your company. Notice the different vibe; first you will feel like an outsider when you see the comic book, Star Wars (or Star Trek), or other gaming character figures on their desks and in their cubicles. The screen savers and the stickers on their laptops are also distinct. We're going out on a limb here, but our guess is that on a similar walk through accounting, legal or for that matter, even the sales department, you aren't seeing any Deadpool or Boba Fett statues. Due to IT's unique culture, one way to keep that staff productive is to not force them into the rigid 9-5 pace of the corporate world.

If we've learned anything from the pandemic about work, we've learned that resources can function at a high level from home without being constantly supervised. Alternatively, after working from home for months, more resources may actually prefer to be in the office than before. Flexibility is key!

Below are a few suggestions about dealing with your resources that might give you a leg up on your competition. Keep in mind that these suggestions come from people who have been in IT since the predotcom era and have worked as consultants for much of that time. We have been in hundreds of companies and seen both good and bad.

1. Ask your staff to describe their ideal working environment. We have all heard this before, but take your team out to lunch, in small groups if the team is large. Ask them directly, "What would your ideal working environment look like?" Listen carefully and then try to make it happen. Even if you can't give them everything they're looking for, your efforts in that direction will go a long way in establishing loyalty and trust. We are going out on a limb, with nearly 100% certainty, that their ideal environment isn't a cubicle farm buried in the basement of some high-rise where they never see the sun. Nor will it be anything cubicle related, especially those short or shared ones where you have no privacy. Whose stupid ideas were those anyway? We don't care about the latest study from some university claiming how these environments enhance creativity; they are just plain dumb. Sorry, we'll save the rest of that rant for another time.

    a. When you arrive at a consensus about an ideal working environment, be that awesome boss that makes it happen!

    b. If you can't make it happen, make sure to get at least something done from their top 10 list and show them that you really tried.

    c. The attitude toward the boss by the peers of a new hire will go a long way in retaining that resource. If you have shown that you will fight for your staff, it will get communicated through the team and new hires.

2. Don't micromanage your rock stars! You know who they are. Even if that top talent is a newbie or a beginner and they don't know their own capabilities yet, they will have the right attitude; they know what they're doing and will work to prove it. Most of the time, it is the drones that need to be micromanaged, and this

is important to keep the organization running. We know there are rock star drones out there somewhere. They probably work in Silicon Valley and make more than the GDP of a small country, but they still need more direction than your star leaders who will drive your success and win you the title of manager of the year. If you provide them with freedom to be creative and the support that shows you are more invested in your team's success instead of your own, they will make you more successful in the long run.

Humans don't fit in easily defined boxes and are not all the same.

3. Freedom and control over their schedule—IT can be tedious! We don't care how much you love your job, especially when it comes to writing code, reviewing log files, and writing documentation. Your resources need to work when it is best for them. For example, Mike likes to write documentation at 10:00 PM in his dark home office while drinking scotch and listening to Jimmy Buffett. For some reason that process just works best for him when it comes to writing documentation. If he had to sit in a cube from 7 AM-4 PM to do the same writing, it would take 3 to 4 times as long and the quality would be nowhere near as high. We are not talking about this book, you're reading, which could never be written in a cube. We are talking about writing Data Security Policy, Information Security Policy, Key Management, etc. You know, the really exciting stuff! Your team members will be most productive when they are working in the surroundings that are most suitable for them.

   a. Allow your people to work in a way and a time where they can maximize their efforts and be most efficient.

b. If you have resources which are night owls, don't make them come in at 7 a.m. because their productivity will be low until at least 10 a.m., when their body clock switches on. If you have resources that work better during non-traditional times, let them work those times. The caveat is if they are needed for an early morning meeting, they need to join but can do so remotely.

c. If you pay attention, you can always tell if your team members are getting their work done. Don't worry so much about people "slacking" when working remotely but point it out if they are.

d. You may also have resources that want to pick up their kids after school or take them to school in the morning. Be sensitive to those situations as well. They may need a hybrid schedule, such as working in the office from 8 AM-2 PM and then remotely from 3:30-7PM. Be flexible and remember that if a team member's family isn't doing well, their productivity in the workplace will suffer.

4. Working remotely—We promised that we were going to get back to this. Gone are the days when your IT staff has to be in the building where your computers are. The servers are most likely in a data center off site now. The exception, of course, would be small shops and help desk resources that need access to the computers of end users, and, obviously, the data center people (all 10 them in a 400,000-square-foot building somewhere).

We should start with the caveat that working remotely is usually earned. You must trust that your resources are actually doing work and know they're not using Mouse Jiggler on their laptop while playing Fortnight. That being said, allowing your trusted resources to work remotely, even two days per week if they want (and not everyone does), will differentiate you from other companies. It will keep them around when another company offers them to work in a cubicle for $10,000

BUILDING AND KEEPING THE TEAM

more in salary. According to findings from a study by Challenger, Gray, and Christmas, the number of Americans relocating for a new job has dwindled during the last decade, a significant change from the late 1980s when more than a third of job seekers were willing to pick up and move for employment. Over the past decade, 10–12 percent of job seekers relocated for work, compared to nearly 20 percent who relocated for employment in the prior decade. This may be due to multiple factors, like real estate costs and companies not paying for relocation. In a job-seeker or buyer's market, why would you move if you don't have to?

5. Working remotely from another city—Due to the scarcity of resources and people being unwilling to relocate, it may be necessary to hire a resource in another city to work for you 100% remotely. We know it sounds scary, but Mike has worked for one of the largest banks in the country, if not the world, and never met his boss or teammates face to face. Still, he did great work. He wasn't the only one it that situation. That bank only had one city where more than one resource from the team inhabited! They even had one guy driving around the country in a big Prevost RV with an Internet satellite dish on top. He was working from wherever he happened to be that day. There are simple ways to make a cohesive team, even in a remote working environment. For example, requiring video conferencing or flying them in for onsite work one week of every month during their probationary period can be highly effective. Get creative with your approach.

6. Team-building exercises—First make sure that you are doing something your team wants to do. You might even consider just letting your team go out on their own, on the company's dime. Determine where they are going to go (bowling, baseball game, paintball, etc.) give them a budget that can be spent at that location and let the team bond without leadership watching over them. This shows that they are trusted within the organization.

7. The less creative but obvious ideas—Keep your compensation and benefits in step with the market, pay for training and/or CPE, and keep your word.

These are just a few suggestions to help retain your staff. Not everyone will stick around because there is a silly hat day, a Hawaiian Shirt Day, casual Fridays, or even allowing.... JEANS and T-shirts instead of business casual (scandalous we know). Every resource is going to be different but if you are creative, establish a comfortable working environment for them, and keep up with the market for pay, you should be able to retain 80% of your resources in the long-term. This will make your job far easier because you will have people you can rely on and trust. The company will be more profitable and you'll be able to make better use of your budget.

So why did you just spend time reading this? Since it can't be the phenomenal writing, it is probably because you have the same problem that we all have: 5 open requisitions for new resources and no good options to hire. Our goal for this chapter was simply to give you a few ideas and help you start thinking about how to maximize successful hiring of new professionals and retaining existing staff longer. For the recruiters out there, maybe you can whisper in the ear of the companies you support and give them a few suggestions about how they can hire and retain good IT and security resources.

> *"He who plants many company culture seeds reaps a great company culture harvest."*
> —Ancient InfoSec Proverb

WHAT'S IN A PROACTIVE CYBERSECURITY PROGRAM?

You now have a solid understanding of cybersecurity fundamentals from a leadership perspective. You also have a smorgasbord of foundational knowledge that will serve you well (and we wish that more people knew), so let's take a deeper dive.

We'll now discuss the common components of a proactive cybersecurity program. Keep in mind that different security professionals will organize plans and present things in different ways. So, if you've seen different requirements or descriptions, *hold on to your britches*. Our objective here is to get to the essence of what an organization should have, be, and do, in order to be considered "proactive."

What will this cost? In reality, good IT shops already have the technical basics of cybersecurity in-house. The real cost will be determined by whether or not senior management commits to a top-down proactive cybersecurity program and if they have a good IT team to help implement the changes. We know that sounds simple but let us explain.

Senior Management Commitment. Why Is It Important? Shouldn't It Be IT Driven?

A proactive cybersecurity posture should be a commitment from Senior Management, not just senior IT management. The reason being is that a true proactive cybersecurity program touches all business units of a company from the CEO on down.

HOW DOES THIS AFFECT THE ENTIRE ORGANIZATION?

Training

One of the keys to proactive cybersecurity is implementing a training program for all users. It should not only teach them what cybersecurity means to the company, but also how to identify risks and help them change behaviors. Additionally, a complete training program will include the proper ways to address phishing and smishing on their work devices; something they can also benefit from in their personal lives. Finally, training about social engineering is also required. Due to the sophistication of the newest generation of firewalls, frontal assaults on enterprises are becoming rare and cybercriminals are turning to social engineering. These attacks take many forms. They can leverage not only email and text but also the telephone, or for a truly valuable target, physical exploitation. In a proactive cybersecurity program, everyone in the organization is required to have adequate security awareness and response training.

Passwords

Another key to proactive cybersecurity is to require users to change their passwords at least quarterly and use strong passwords, which means they are longer than 8 characters, preferably 12 to 14 and up, and include special characters, upper and lowercase letters, and non-sequential numbers. Gone are the days of using "0ctober01" or "Pa$$w0rd". Passwords should look more like this "_6u^njc72A<jaU#p", which is easier and more realistic if you have a password manager deployed on all machines. Another way to prevent a hard password from being on a sticky note under the keyboard is to recommend that each user sets a phrase that they can remember, with number and letter substitution, like "B!g_Br0wnD0g$." Hard passwords must be a requirement for everyone in the company.

Two-Factor or Multi-Factor Authentication (MFA)

Whenever possible, even if you are using single sign on, implement MFA for access to the network and critical resources. This will be an adjustment but there are many plug-and-play options that can be utilized for network and critical data access.

Decommission Deprecated Hardware and Software

Whenever we discuss strong passwords, we remember issues where companies had restrictions on passwords due to legacy hardware and software. This was mainly an issue with old mainframe systems running homegrown antiquated programs. Some companies were more committed to the ease of access for their users and kept all passwords in a format that would work with the mainframes, such as "Wallys1." Eight characters, with a capital letter at the beginning, a number at the end, and no deviations. Some organizations were smart enough to realize that less than 10% of their employees accessed the mainframe, so rather than requiring everyone to use a weak password to support the mainframe, they would have those that required access use an additional mainframe password or use a jump box for access. If you are still using deprecated hardware and or software, you should consider phasing it out as quickly as possible. If you can't get rid of those systems, work with your security team on developing compensating controls to protect the vulnerable devices.

Proactive Patching

Whenever possible, unless it will cause harm to an existing system, install patches on your systems when they become available. This is a simple statement but, in many organizations, depending on user location and infrastructure complexity, it is not a simple task. For more sophisticated infrastructure, running complex and/or homegrown applications, it is necessary to test patches in a testing environment to ensure they don't break anything and interrupt productivity. Sounds simple, right? The problem we often see is that many organizations don't have a dedicated test environment that properly matches what they have in production, that is if they have one at all. In other situations, the current resources are simply not available to test and patch. Patch management could be a full-time job depending on the size of your organization.

User location also creates an expanded level of difficulty in some organizations. It is simple to push patches to users but it becomes far more challenging for a geographically dispersed user population with remote users. Fortunately, there are some tools on the market that will automate the patching process for remote and geographic users. Those will require a significant initial investment, so it might be time to go talk with senior management.

Vulnerability Management Program (VMP)

Vulnerability management programs can actually save you time when it comes to patching and remediation of vulnerabilities. A VMP will require proactive scanning, both internally and externally, which will require some investment for a scanning solution *("Hello again Senior Management")*. Fortunately, the marketplace is literally flooded with them. They all are based on the same CVE risk database, although they may vary in interpretation of the data and the risk ranking. If implemented properly, a VMP will take much of the busywork and guesswork out of patch management. In the VMP Plan, you can prioritize patching based on risk, as illustrated in the table below. This will allow you to prioritize your patching.

Remediation SLAs

Severity	Remediation Timeline
Critical	7 days*
High	30 days*

Medium	90 days*
Low	180 days*

In addition to the table above, there is an added element of the VMP that should be implemented and that is risk-based patching. For example, if a scanner rates a vulnerability a 10 (or 5 in some cases) which is considered critical, we recommend you investigate the vulnerability and ask the following questions:

- Is there an exploit for this vulnerability? In many situations, a critical vulnerability will exist but it might not have a corresponding known exploit. In which case the risk can be downgraded to High.

- Do my compensating controls mitigate the risk? The easiest way to find this out is to ask your security team. Failing that, you can consult the CVE Calculator, which is tied to the National Vulnerability Database (NVD). The CVE Calculator is a risk calculator where you plug in your CVE with compensating controls and it comes up with an actual risk score. This score will provide you a better understanding of the true risks associated with the vulnerability.

Visit http://resources.cyberrants.com for links to the NIST CVE calculator and other materials.

A proper VMP Plan will dramatically improve security and make patching more economical in time and resources.

> *"He who believes he does not have data worth stealing also pees upside down into the wind."*
>
> —Ancient Infosec Proverb

Data Management

Data management and protection are the primary reasons for proactive cybersecurity. The strategy should be based on the CIA Triad of Confidentiality, Integrity, and Availability. Whether the data is client, transactional, or Intellectual Property (IP), the goal is to keep the bad guys from stealing data from under noses and out of our systems. The first step in data management is data classification. You have to know what you have and what is critical in order to protect it properly.

Further adding to the data classification challenge is the need to retain data for compliance reasons. The flip side of that is knowing when and how to purge data that you are no longer required to keep. Sadly, many companies have become data hoarders and this creates its own set of issues. Outdated data can be a liability and it will impact a company financially in the long run.

Don't be a data hoarder. Dispose of data that you are no longer required to keep. It's a liability, not an asset.

Data classification can generally be classified in three categories: Public, Confidential, and Highly Confidential. Some people add a fourth category for PCI or HIPAA compliance but in reality, it is just another form of highly confidential data.

Why are we talking about this? By identifying what type of data the organization holds, you will know how to properly protect it and how it should be accessed to ensure that it remains secure. Confidential data requires many different controls, comparatively to public data (like the stuff on your website). In reality, who cares if a cybercriminal steals

WHATS IN A PROACTIVE CYBERSECURITY PROGRAM?

information meant to be publicly available? It is public for a reason so locking it in an encrypted database behind multiple firewalls isn't critical.

The private and confidential data is what needs to be securely stored and access needs to be restricted in order to ensure the bad guys don't steal the "keys to the kingdom." Confidential data needs to be stored on dedicated servers, where possible, and on a segregated secure virtual local area network (VLAN) with restricted access. It should be encrypted both at rest and in transit. It can be further protected using access control, jump boxes, secret server, and many other options.

Sadly, you can have a great tech solution for securing data but without other controls, it only takes one user to plug in a found USB drive that turns out to be loaded with malware, and "BOOM!" all efforts were wasted.

There are many ways to securely store data. Just don't put an encrypted database on a flat network and think it's okay.

How do you address the human element? Training, processes, and procedures. Your people must be trained on how to properly handle confidential and private data. There must be processes and standards for data storage, transmission, and handling. Data access needs to be restricted based on the lowest privileges required, ensuring that users can only access what they need for their daily operations. Checks and balances need to be in place to ensure that policies, processes, and standards are followed.

The biggest risk to the enterprise is always the human.

The last thing you want to do, and sadly we have seen this happen, is to let a developer, on a temporary contract, load a database of confidential data on their laptop so they can work over the weekend, just because the organization won't allow contractors a VPN access. Confidential data should stay securely in production environments. It does not belong on laptops or in development environments.

> *"One who has a flat network has given their treasure map to the enemy."*
> —Ancient Infosec Proverb

Network Management

Gone are the days when the only goal of network teams was to keep the network up and running. Their mission has changed to keep systems up, running, and secure. This can be accomplished in many ways. We all still want 99.9999% uptime as a goal, but security cannot be sacrificed for uptime in today's environment. The network and security teams need to work together in a proactive security program as one force to protect the enterprise. However, there needs to be separation of duties since both teams, at times, have divergent goals.

Firewall Management

Security needs to have the final say for any changes to the firewall. We know that sounds like a dictatorship, but the fact is, IT is not a democracy and it shouldn't be run like one. That being said, there needs to be flexibility by the security team to ensure that the business can meet its goals, serve its customers, and function properly. We all can't live with air-gapped networks where the only user privilege is read and not write. However, as part of the change management process (we will touch on that in more details later), security needs to review and sign off on any and all firewall changes, prior to implementation. This is in order to ensure there is minimal risk to the environment and that all changes are documented properly.

Additional Key Points

- Blacklist malicious IPs, and those from unverified/obfuscated sources (TOR, unapproved VPNs, etc.)
- Implement VLANs and secure your data in a secure VLAN. There is no excuse for a flat network.
- If you use wireless networks, monitor your Wireless Access Points (WAPs) and periodically check for rogue access points.
- Do not allow Bring Your Own Devices (BYOD) on the production network, be it wired or wireless. If necessary, provide a guest network for personal devices.
- Implement MAC filtering and whitelisting when possible.

PREVENTATIVE MEDICINE

Penetration Tests (Pen Tests)

From a cybersecurity perspective, some "preventive medicine" includes penetration tests, risk assessments, third-party audits, and Business Impact Assessments (BIAs).

We will touch on penetration testing extensively later in this book but in relation to proactive cybersecurity. Keeping up with the medical theme, this is the equivalent of getting a physical. For example, a black box external pen test of a specific subnet or application can be compared to a simple physical exam, where they listen to your heart and lungs and draw some blood. The more invasive option, a full on "turn your head and cough" while checking from head to toe, would be an internal or external pen test, and perhaps even white box application testing. In short, a pen test will provide you with a status varying in depth, depending on what type of pen test you chose, either for your entire enterprise or for a part of it. Penetration tests allow a third party to identify your vulnerabilities, based on actual risk, while providing you a snapshot of what a cybercriminal could find to exploit. This is important, from a proactive perspective, because it will allow you to address these issues before a cybercriminal with malintent finds the weakness and exploits them to steal your data.

Always remember that cybercriminals around the world are working full time, even during a pandemic, to steal from others. Like the Terminator, they don't stop for holidays or because a company performs a vital function in society. This notion is easily supported by looking at the number of attempted hacks, phishing schemes, and fraud targeting hospitals and medical workers during the pandemic.

There is another type of pen test that doesn't get the attention that it should. This is the physical penetration test. This test will see a human or group of humans attempt to hack your security or people physically. It could be as simple as sneaking past the security desk by pretending to be a delivery person, to working hard enough to pull critical data out of targeted individuals by using social media, or even by simply befriending someone to gather sensitive information. These tests will often demonstrate the complacency of the workforce to strangers or issues related with multiple entrances to a facility when only the main door is guarded.

Audits, Business Continuity Plans, Risk Assessments, and More

A later chapter is dedicated to compliance, which involves an audit component. However, what is often overlooked by those that do not have a compliance requirement is the proactive step of a voluntary audit of their IT environment against a security framework like NIST SP 800-171 or CIS Controls. These audits will provide management with a clear idea of their real risk. With the heightened risk due to cybercriminals, it is important that you use a third party, at least annually, to review your environment holistically, from the technical aspects to your policies and procedures. In order to have an effective Incident Response (IR) or Disaster Recovery (DR) document, it is important to have a Business Continuity Plan (BCP). There are formal BCPs and informal BCPs but a plan is necessary, regardless of type. If done properly, a BCP will help you identify critical resources, both human and technology. The BCP will tell you what systems need to be restored first and what resources are required to support them in the event of a disaster.

Case in point, what happens if there is a pandemic and everyone has to work from home? Can your VPN support the bandwidth? What about people who don't have laptops? What is critical to keep the company running and what can be left out until it is possible to resume normal operations? We don't mean to make light of the pandemic by using it as an example, but we all should ask, how many businesses were prepared for what we have witnessed, from both a human and economic perspective?

> *"Those who don't have a BCP plan, plan to fail."*
> —Ancient Infosec Proverb

Process and Documentation

This is every IT professional's favorite subject! Yay documentation! This is a much-maligned topic, which is too often avoided, but documenting processes, policies, procedures, standards, and systems is critical to proactive cybersecurity. The appropriate Governance, Regulatory, and Compliance (GRC) document can help you protect your environment, your data, and provide a roadmap to recovery. The simplest processes, such as the onboarding of new users or requests for new keyboards, will simplify the management of the enterprise, just as the rules around making changes to the firewall will protect the security of your environment.

A piece that is often forgotten is the proper diagramming and documentation of your systems (Networks, Servers, and applications). There are many great tools out there, like Visio, that will assist you in creating a graphical view of your enterprise as a whole, and applications that will map your environment for you. Some of us are old school and prefer to draw it up ourselves using Visio but that is just personal preference. The diagrams that you create are critical to your disaster recovery (DR) and restoring operations, should something catastrophic occur. They are also critical to your change management process.

Change Management

Change management has varying degrees of complexity, but all versions of change management have the same goal. It is to ensure that any change to the environment doesn't negatively impact the enterprise as a whole. Establishing a strong change management process requires documentation of the modifications, change windows, backout plans, and system documentation. This will help even the smallest company strengthen security and stability in their environment.

Final Thoughts About Proactive Cybersecurity

Proactive cybersecurity allows you to create a great defense that will mitigate the attacks from the bad guys. If you build an enterprise with defense in depth and maintain your hardware and software to current standards, maintain a strong change management program to minimize risk, mitigate the human risk through policy, process, procedure, standard, and training, you have a very good chance of blunting cybercriminal attacks. You will be a hard-enough target that cybercriminals will be more likely to give up and go for the low-hanging fruit, another organization that hasn't put the time and effort into securing their environment. Should you get breached, your current BCP, IR and DR Plans will provide the ability to quickly rebuild your environment. We don't need to hack back to beat the cybercriminals, we simply need to build our enterprises strong enough to deter attacks. At the very least, we should be harder to breach than the next company on their list.

BUILDING A SECURITY CONSCIOUS CULTURE

The human element is the most vulnerable aspect of an organization's security posture but can also be your strongest defensive measure. As humans, we cannot be configured like machines, sorting information based purely on logic. Cyber criminals understand that people are vulnerable so they use techniques to manipulate our emotions and gain access to data that would otherwise remain confidential. This practice is called "social engineering" and some refer to it as "human hacking."

Building a security-conscious culture is a critical asset to an organization's security program, brand credibility, and longevity. Most find that increasing their team's attention to detail also creates a significant improvement in company culture and efficiency of operations.

Unfortunately, organizational culture is not changed in a single activity or exercise. It is transformed slowly over time. The good news is that building a security-conscious culture is one of the most budget-friendly processes in building a proactive cybersecurity program.

These are the standard steps we recommend to build your staff awareness training program:

1. Leadership Decision & Commitment

You can see by now that it all starts with leadership. Most companies failing to build effective cybersecurity programs are those failing to make the decision at the leadership level, then see it through. Your staff always looks to leadership and will mirror the actions they see. If your leaders are sending documents with sensitive information over email, leaving their computers unlocked when they step away, and using company computers for personal use, the staff will behave in the same manner.

2. Determine Special Attack Vectors and Compliance Requirements

Every industry and company has its own types of data and computing resources that cyber criminals will target for specific reasons. You may be in the healthcare industry, subject to HIPAA compliance, and hold millions of Protected Health Information (PHI) records. Cyber criminals target this information heavily, which is something to be considered when building your training program. Manufacturing companies rely on computing resources in specific networks to maintain production. Financial services companies hold sensitive information about customers and transactions. Regardless of your industry, always ask the question, *"What is our sensitive information or computing resource that would cause tremendous harm if it was in control of anyone outside our company?"* Keep the answers in mind so you can make your staff aware of the critical nature of these assets and how to protect them.

3. Determine Level(s) of Commitment

There is a fine line between keeping security top-of-mind and letting the messaging become "noise" in each team member's busy schedule. It is important to determine the appropriate amount of training without taking so much time that you experience a reduction in productivity. Consider how much time you believe is appropriate on an annual basis and we'll discuss frequency later as we get into security program maintenance. At a bare minimum, we recommend one hour of total security awareness training for each staff member, spread throughout the year.

Not all divisions or roles within a company need to have the same level of awareness. For a large organization, consider the

BUILDING A SECURITY CONSCIOUS CULTURE

implementation of training programs per division, department, or level of access to critical computing resources or information.

4. Establish a Baseline

You will need to measure where your organization's staff awareness stands today in order to measure improvement. Much like the technical aspects of security, this benchmarking process starts with a test. Before announcing a security awareness initiative to the entire staff, start by launching a phishing test campaign. The initial phishing test should be configured to send a variety of test phishing emails to all team members in the company. When an individual opens a test phishing email, they will be logged as doing so. When they click a link or send a reply, the action will also be logged. With these metrics, you'll quickly see the level of awareness of the staff throughout the organization. Upon completion, you'll have figures showing the percentage of opens and clicks, as well as details on the emails and links that fooled users. These figures will serve as baseline metrics and the intent is to improve them over time with training.

This type of testing can be completed with one of many automated cloud-based platforms on the market. A few of those platforms include KnowBe4, Wombat, Sophos Phish Threat, and Barracuda PhishLine.

Depending on the size and resources of your organization, you may also decide to engage a firm to conduct vishing or even physical intrusion testing. Vishing is the process cyber criminals use to elicit sensitive information over the phone. It involves calling a company and using social engineering techniques to talk unsuspecting employees into revealing information that may be used to support malicious activity. Physical intrusion testing involves gaining access to a company's headquarters or remote sites in order to tamper with or plant malware on the company's technology devices. These activities can be conducted professionally by independent security firms like Silent Sector.

5. Announce the Secure Culture Initiative

To refer back to Step 1, it all starts with leadership support. You should explain the importance of cybersecurity and why it is critical for your organization. You might even refer to results of the security baseline that was set during the initial testing.

Of course, never call out a person individually for clicking on a phishing link or make an example of any team member. This will only cause fear and distrust. Instead, explain your intent to help the staff understand and recognize cyber threats in order to protect not only the company, but themselves and loved ones. When individuals are equipped with information and awareness to protect themselves at a personal level, the same heightened awareness will benefit their activities in the work environment.

6. Implement the Initial Training Campaign

The first cybersecurity awareness training campaign will generally be the most robust. We recommend that all staff receive the initial training, in the same timeframe, and include that training as part of the onboarding process for future team members.

Forty-five minutes is generally sufficient for the first training and about the maximum amount of effective training time in a single sitting. Awareness training can usually be distributed through the same platforms used for phishing tests, such as those mentioned above. These training and phishing platforms have robust libraries of training content so you can choose to distribute information relevant to your organization.

A good initial awareness training session for your staff would generally include a combination of the following topics:

- Phishing
- Social Engineering
- Safe Passwords

- Clean Desk and Other Company Policies
- Unauthorized USB Drives
- Keyloggers
- Privileged User Access
- Public Wi-Fi Safety
- Physical Security
- Social Media
- Current Situational Threats

7. Maintain & Improve Your Security Conscious Culture

With baseline metrics established and the initial training complete, you are ready to focus on developing further awareness and prevention of malicious activities.

Frequency is critical in keeping any important matter top-of-mind. The old approach, with the annual one-hour security presentation, is simply not effective to maintain vigilance and keep up with new threats.

One of our recommendations is to conduct an organization-wide phishing test every month. Those who continue to open phishing emails and click on links will be tracked and can receive remedial training. Your organization's security program should include a policy and simple method for employees to report potentially malicious emails. This may be a button on their email client, such as Outlook, or simply forwarding the suspicious email to a dedicated address.

Training should be conducted on a quarterly basis at a minimum. After the initial training, you can break training sessions down to shorter segments so they don't interfere with productivity or create frustration. Fifteen to twenty minutes is generally a good module length for quarterly sessions. Some readily available modules will include slide shows, video sessions, TV-like series, games, quizzes, or a combination of materials designed to make the material engaging and memorable.

RULES OF A SECURITY CONSCIOUS CULTURE

1. Do Not Punish: Never punish or give anyone a hard time for reporting suspected malicious activity, even if it turns out to be a perfectly legitimate situation.

2. Develop Confidence, Not Fear: Fear mongering techniques force employees to tune out of learning opportunities and conceal mistakes that may lead to compromise. This is why you want to develop a culture based on confidence, not fear. Empower your team with education and equip them to react appropriately. It is important for them to know that reported errors and incidents will not result in punishment or dismissal.

3. Be the Example: Leaders must practice what they preach. Every leader must follow the same or even more stringent standards. With leaders being the prime targets for cyber criminals, it is critical to take extra precautions. When a leader cuts corners, their team will follow the example.

Development of a security-conscious culture is one of the most critical aspects of any cyber risk management program. It is simple and highly effective. While it takes planning, time, and commitment to implement effectively, it is also one of the most budget-friendly aspects of your security program. A security-conscious culture will not only prevent breaches, it will improve your staff's confidence, your company's brand credibility, and support the longevity of the organization.

CYBER RISK ASSESSMENTS AND PENETRATION TESTING

It's time to put your "bad guy hat" on and start thinking like a cybercriminal. You are about to learn more than you probably ever wanted to know about cyber risk assessments and penetration testing. Why? Because it's that important. It is essential to understand how risk is assessed and get to know the nuances. Thinking like a bad guy will not only help you recognize security shortcomings so they can be fixed, it will also help you understand what testers and auditors are looking for in your organization.

> *"Great security without testing is no better than an educated guess."*
> —Ancient Infosec Proverb

We'll cover a wide range of considerations such as the risks of penetration testing, how they are conducted, what should be included, what budget to expect, physical security testing, and industry jargon. Some people may put different meanings to industry jargon but we'll describe terms in the way we believe they should be defined.

A strong understanding of how risk is assessed will help you make better decisions while reducing wasted effort and budget throughout the cyber risk management process.

This is where the rubber meets the road…

CYBER RISK ASSESSMENT VS. PENETRATION TEST

As we define it, cyber risk assessment is the evolution of the modern penetration test. With the current threat vectors currently being used, like advanced email phishing, smishing, SIM-swapping, physical security bypass, badge cloning and operating system patching weaknesses, it's no wonder that the common penetration test offered as a service would need to evolve. They should provide a more comprehensive understanding of the risk vectors for an organization's technology assets.

In the past, penetration testing was commonly referring to the activities around attempting to identify the weakness in built-in or bolted on software for technology targets. (e.g. Windows servers or web applications, the business-blogging site, exposed remote access servers, etc.) These software weaknesses, commonly referred to as "vulnerabilities," contain various levels of misuse. Some vulnerabilities can be applied and leveraged in a manner that could close a company's doors for good and destroy personal and business reputations across the known digital world.

The cyber risk assessment covers more than the classic penetration test and, in most cases, is more appropriate for today's complex environments. Spot-checking specific areas, like your production web server or your externally exposed IP block, will not provide a holistic view of all the potential risk to your business from a cyber threat perspective. Instead of spot-checking, focus on the entire organization's technology dependencies and the humans that operate and administer those technologies. A cyber risk assessment identifies all areas of business cyber risk, from the human element to the technologies and software the business depends on, whereas the classic penetration test focuses on one or two specific areas (e.g. external web app and/or network).

Please note that companies will occasionally use the term "cyber risk assessment" to mean a purely non-technical, "paper review" of a security program. While this is one necessary part of assessing risk, it is not a holistic or thorough approach. In other words, it's not just about what you see on paper. What really matters is what the cyber criminals see. Both technical and non-technical evaluations are needed to fully understand the risk profile.

THINK LIKE THE BAD GUY

Thinking like the bad guy will assist you in understanding all the risk areas that need to be assessed. The theory of attack has always been simple. Find a weakness and exploit it. Every successful military strategist in history has used this strategy. The theory is applicable regardless if the target is a human, groups of humans, or the technologies they use and depend on. At this very moment, cybercriminals are attempting to find weaknesses with both ongoing network/web scanning and phishing/smishing campaigns.

The ability to identify weaknesses in electronic devices has long been a revered craft practiced by a dedicated few and one that is too often used for villainy. The defensive response is also simple. Be proactive and find the weaknesses that cause risk to your business first, before others outside your organization do. The outcome of a cyber risk assessment or a penetration test is to find solutions that will strengthen any identified weaknesses, especially the critical ones.

Some of the remediation or solutions will be simple, like patching your operating system regularly. Others will include ongoing maintenance, like training your staff to identify malicious emails that could contain malware and remote access toolkits. All the security technologies in the world can't protect a human from making a mistake, ignoring alerts and allowing the bypass of all your expensive technology controls. Cyclical and ongoing training is most necessary to combat this sort of mistake. Remember to think like a bad guy when it comes to understanding the security controls you need to assess for your business. If you don't have a security team in house or outsourced, then pull in your lead technical person and ask them if they are aware of any avenues of attack for any of the technologies that are presented to the public network spaces. They will be your first line of information when it comes to the technologies exposed to public networks and if any misconfigurations or outdated software exists on these systems.

We see organizations that refute and challenge any cybersecurity practices suggested to them by either qualified internal employees or 3rd party experts. Then we see them get breached. To quote the Joker from the latest movie; "You get what you deserve." Sorry, not sorry.

STANDARDS FOR CYBER RISK ASSESSMENTS AND PENETRATION TESTING

An organization that does even a small part of its business over the World Wide Web or Internet of Things, incurs a specific amount of risk due to their dependence on some technologies and a public interconnected infrastructure. The common excuse of "*I don't have anything cyber-criminals want*" is over. If you have computing power, even in the form of a home grade laptop or a personal smartphone, let us assure you, you are most wanted. At the very least, there are those who would want to abuse your computing power to do things such as mining cryptocurrency or use your computer host as a decoy for dubious activities, leading federal or local cyber hounds back to your company's network. Maybe you have juicy data, like credit cards, PII, defense trade secrets or genetic data. The amount of risk will be dependent on several factors of your cyber-based activities as a business and the types of resources and data you maintain.

A cyber risk assessment should be conducted in a manner that addresses six specific target areas. The risk is determined from the amount of dependency your business has in any of the five areas below and their relation to each other.

1. Hardware dependencies (desktops, laptops, servers, virtualization systems, routers, switches, load balancers, firewalls, storage area networks, mobile devices like phones, tablets and printers).
2. Network dependencies (the external and internal network architecture used for the business to include wireless).
3. Software Dependencies (operating systems like Windows or Linux, database systems, web applications, software as a service).
4. Physical security dependencies (building access points, physical access technologies, security guards, security systems).
5. Human dependencies (the entirety of your employee base, contractors included).
6. Data dependencies (the data types you require to conduct business operations).

> *"If a technology is publicly accessible, the wise one remembers that cybercriminals are part of the public."*
> —Ancient InfoSec Proverb

You may not be able to find a vendor that offers a total perspective of your cyber risk, depending on budgetary limitations. If you only have the option of a penetration test (e.g. network or web application), make sure you are targeting the test toward your critical, publicly exposed, environments. Targeting these areas will give you the best "drive-by" attacker protection and bang for your buck. Now let's discuss protocol for penetration testing. There is a standardized protocol for conducting these tests. However, some may use different names for the same methods. Our protocol for both technical penetration testing and physical intrusion testing is as generally as follows:

1. Reconnaissance

This involves information gathering of the target environments and humans. We perform open-source intelligence, in addition to the technology asset discovery, collecting as much information as possible. We check dark web spaces and frequently used marketplaces for exploits and compromised data that may belong to our client. We review culture and dress codes for ways to provide a focused physical risk assessment for our clients.

2. Vulnerability Identification (Technology & Human)

Social engineering and phishing will provide information that will assist in vulnerability identification related to the human element. During this phase, technologies like Qualys or Rapid7 Nexpose are also used to scan for technology and software vulnerabilities. We will often look for signs of misuse or abuse from employees of certain controls, like tailgating.

3. Attack Surface Identification

This consists of identifying the areas that are weak and which could be taken advantage of with scripts to inject or phishing attachments that a user clicks on. Often signage is not enough to prevent some employees from allowing others to tailgate through controlled areas. If this is the case, we can leverage it in our physical bypass testing.

4. Exploitation

This is the act of exploiting the weaknesses identified in earlier stages. With a big smile, a box of donuts and a malicious thumb drive, we will enter your place of business and deploy the thumb drive to as many hosts as possible. Similar results can be accomplished by sending a phishing email with a malicious attachment or running a script against a Windows server to take advantage of a critical vulnerability in SMB/RDP for remote technology access. We will also hijack internal wireless networks to intercept session cookies that can then be replayed or traffic diverted to fake login pages that record keystrokes.

5. Credential Hijacking

This is a process to obtain credentials in an arbitrary manner. Once an exploit has successfully executed against the target, usernames and password hashes can be exposed to unauthorized persons with access. Frequency copiers can be used to gain access by cloning existing badges or creating badges from the reader itself. Finding online images of an employee wearing a badge can also allow us to create a pretty good fake badge.

6. Unauthorized Access Validation

Validate the successful enumeration of an account and test it to make sure it works on the exploited system. This could mean RC4 hashes or SNMP community strings. In physical intrusion testing, this involves making sure the fake badge works or that we've successfully social engineered our way past a controlled point of entry.

7. Escalation of Access

Also known as "privilege escalation," escalation of access means to move from a place of low permissions or access to a place of greater permissions and ultimate access, like an Admin user account. This might be done by getting the administrator account hash and breaking it. It can also be the social engineering into the client's onsite data center by carrying and connecting a testing thumb drive.

8. Access Persistence

We create a method to ensure long-term access. This could be by creating a new account with elevated privileges and using an existing corporate VPN profile or a meterpreter session to allow the tester remote access at any time. In a physical intrusion test, we might deploy an SSH Server from a thumb drive so we can establish a remote connection later.

9. Deep-Set Validation

This is often referred to as "pivoting." It is the process of ensuring permanent occupancy and discovery of all other internal systems, networks and data. Once we can connect through SSH back to the network, we can deploy tools to scan other internal resources. As long as internal routing permits, the entire network and systems footprint can be discovered. We can then try to exploit other systems that may allow us to persist our stay and continue to explore for data.

10. Evidence Presentation

Evidence is key in ensuring due diligence in the testing. Once something is exploited, evidence should be gathered to validate the successful proof of concept used. These details should be present in the final report. We generally provide this in the form of screenshots or video files (screen recording).

RISKS OF CONDUCTING A PENETRATION TEST OR CYBER RISK ASSESSMENT

Regardless of whether you own the company, provide sales support, or manage the business technologies, you will eventually come across the requirement for a penetration test. Maybe the request for a penetration test report came from one of your potential customers through a security questionnaire or maybe it was a direct ask from an auditor working for a big firm that is attempting to purchase your business. It could be that you have already been breached and you are now attempting to identify your weaknesses by using a penetration test. Perhaps you've decided to be proactive and download the PCI data security standard in order to align your business to a security framework and gain a competitive advantage against others in your market space. You might have come across requirement 11.3 that asks for internal and external penetration testing and you said to yourself *"that's something I should get done. I wonder what's involved?"* Nah, that wouldn't be a realistic scenario but if that is the reason you are here reading this section, welcome to the 1% club!

Penetration testing is like inspecting a toilet with a microscope and reporting on the filth identified. You probably won't like what you find but don't take it too personally.

There are risks in everything we do. Penetration testing is no different. We hope to help bring some of these risks into the light so they may be understood and most importantly, expected. While penetration testing and cyber risk assessments are proactive cybersecurity strategies, they are not without consequence. It doesn't matter if your reason for getting a penetration test is driven by a compliance requirement or a proactive opportunity that you are seeking, there are certainly some negative aspects that you can expect to occur as a byproduct of the testing. Negatives can usually be turned into positives and while there are some risks to be aware of, they are certainly stepping stones on the road to a mature cybersecurity program.

1. Risk: Discovery of Massive Amounts of Vulnerabilities

Penetration testing methods will cover a deep discovery of your technologies and humans. The results of the test will portray opportunistic attack surfaces relevant to the scope of work. In unattended environments, this could mean tens of thousands or even more vulnerabilities that are critical and can be taken advantage of by cybercriminals. Now that you are aware that you have vulnerabilities, you are compelled to remediate them or suffer at the hands of your compliance overlords. Or worse, you get hit by a drive-by cybercriminal who finds the easy way to drop ransomware on your systems due to one of these identified vulnerabilities.

Some of the findings may require more work than anticipated. For example, you might find that you have to re-architect a portion of your web application or you could learn that your firewall software is no longer supported after attempting to upgrade it to solve a vulnerability. Recurring penetration tests will ultimately require that you keep hardware and software, including networking components, updated to stay ahead of threats.

Continuous vulnerability scanning helps to increase configuration security confidence by identifying and validating system states at a high frequency. However, you plan to accomplish the continuous vulnerability scanning (deploy and manage onsite or outsource service), you will need to allocate a budget for both technology and professionals with the appropriate expertise.

Risk Mitigation: Proactive Scanning and Patching.

> *"The cybersecurity professional is much like a roofer. Preventing and repairing leaks is a way of life."*
> —Ancient InfoSec Proverb

If you are required to conduct a penetration test, before you pay for one, you should ask your teams to begin installing the latest patches for all technology systems and software. This will get you ahead of any vulnerability scanning that will occur as part of the penetration test and may close much of your attack surface.

If you are feeling proactive, download the free vulnerability scanner Open VAS or get yourself a trial version of a major vendor like Qualys, Nessus or Rapid7. The deployment process is simple, only requiring you to possess a dedicated machine with virtualization software running, like Vbox. You can install the virtual machine version of the trial software and scan a portion of your enterprise to get a baseline understanding of what misconfigurations exist. This is certainly not a replacement for the penetration test, but it will give you some idea of the items that may come up and what the post-testing work will look like.

2. Risk: Discovery of Active or Previous Breaches

The penetration test may uncover accounts and services that you may not be aware of. Sometimes these tests will uncover massive holes in the network and applications. Some of these holes may have been previously used or some may still be actively used by cybercriminals to access your environment. For example, if the penetration tester finds out that you are allowing SSH out to the public networks and this is not something that you or your technical teams use as part of a management capability, then you may have some further investigating to do. The enumeration of accounts will give you lists of accounts on systems, some you may expect to see, like the accounts of your sysadmins and the users of the system, but there is also a chance that you will see an account that you don't recognize and which doesn't follow your standard naming conventions. The tester may find the database for your web application is running default credentials and when walking the directory structure, identifies a compressed version of the database. If your DBAs are using the standard backup methods, then finding a tar ball or .zip of the database will usually mean that someone unauthorized also found it, compressed it and moved it out to review the dataset safely at a later time. Identifying high ports while testing your systems could mean that you have an active malware compromise and it is calling out to their command and control's servers. Something usually happening over specific high ports.

Risk Mitigation: There is not one.

If you have had a breach, then the damage is already done and knowing about it after the fact means you have even fewer options. Remnants of a breach can be exposed when conducting a penetration test. For example, a database left exposed and the server is showing signs of recent output and compression of that database, along with an odd IP address in the logs, indicates the possibility of a past or active compromise. If a breach has occurred and you conduct a forensic investigation on the technologies which also comes back with a high probability rating, let us hope you have cyber insurance to help you with some of the cost of remediation. *Do not have a breach, ever.* That's as plain and simple as we can put it.

3. Risk: Possible Denial of Services (Self-Inflicted)

These tests attempt to inject arbitrary code and commands to your systems' active and listening sockets in the hopes they are parsed into memory and either: A—Offer an exploitable surface of attack or B—Validate the absence of an exploitable surface of attack.

While these tests are occurring, weak technologies may suffer at the hand of the tools. Ensure your systems are not in a frail hardware resource state when these tests are conducted or you may be restarting services and in the worst case, rebuilding systems and databases. When using denial of service techniques, the tester may take down your SSO website and it may not operate normally again without a service restart (not that we know that from our own experience or anything). If you are using auth tokens for your APIs, then the use of authenticated fuzzing methods may render a lot of junk data to your error log stores, which will require that you purge logs and restart services.

Risk Mitigation: Test During Out of Band Hours.

These tests can hit hard at times and going full tilt with a service may end up causing the denial of services, like testing for slow post. To mitigate this risk, you can test during out of band hours. Test during the times of the week that your business has the lowest level of activity coursing through its technologies. This could mean on the weekends or during the early hours of the morning.

You can also use a like-for-like production environment for the testing. This will limit the interference that may be experienced on the production services. However, the environment tested must be like-for-like, meaning an exact replica of the production environment. Otherwise, the penetration test should be conducted against the production services first, then on all other environments. This is to give the best risk model against viable services and data. Remember, you want to scan everything external, production and lower environments that are exposed to the public network fabric. If you are only looking at production externally, you could be missing misconfigurations that are often plaguing the lower testing realms.

Knowing that vulnerabilities in the infrastructure exist is like knowing the grass needs to be cut. It doesn't matter until something is done about it. Completing the task requires the actions of going outside, getting the gas can, filling up the lawnmower, and mowing the grass. If you're busy, just pull out your pocket book to pay the neighbor's kid to do it.

4. Risk: Awareness of Risk Now Requires Resolve

Most will state that the biggest risk of a penetration test is the postmortem budget. If you have been a good cybersecurity practitioner and your business follows your cybersecurity strategy and roadmap, then most, if not all of your penetration tests, come back with an A+ score card and a report that reflects highly on your ability to narrow the attack surface and reduce risk. The only cost you will suffer is the cost of the testing to validate your good security configurations. For everyone else, the penetration test and accompanying vulnerability report may reveal just how bad things really are, which means no more plausible deniability.

You are now going to be compelled to remediate the findings and some items may indicate a requirement for new technologies or processes and the people to manage those technologies and processes. Make sure you are prepared to pull out your company checkbook and start signing checks to cover the shortfalls. If you want to reduce risk to your business, its employees, and 3rd party customers or affiliates, then you will need to budget for closing the gaps identified in the penetration test, especially the serious ones.

Plausible deniability is not a cyber risk management strategy. Even in today's environment, we still hear about the occasional executive who "doesn't want to know."

Those that ignore the critical findings on the reports will often cease to have a company to worry about within a few years. Remember, cybercriminals are continuously scanning the public networks in search of juicy data or companies that have simply decided to go live with a bunch of misconfigurations baked right in. It's safe to say that cybercriminals are conducting unauthorized penetration testing around the clock on businesses without their unawareness. We don't want to sound cliché, but don't end up being a statistic. Remediate all critical findings and reduce risk as much as possible to make your organization a hard target. This is going to cost money, time, and more often than not, both.

Risk Mitigation: Request for budget
and strategize for manpower needs.

If you have inherited the information technology department, or you are the new CISO, you'll need to be making headway in getting enough budget to keep the existing tech updated regularly and have the tools to implement basic security controls, like endpoint security for all laptops, desktops and servers. By understanding how many systems and servers you need to keep updated and secured, you can get a ballpark idea of the cost for endpoint security suites. Ask for pricing from a few major vendors of the controls you are looking to apply. This will help prepare your future request to leadership. You could do this post breach, but the cost will be far higher due to expedited deployment times and so is the stress to implement.

5. Risk: Data Loss by Using Offshore Resources for the Penetration Test

It's now imperative to only use cybersecurity firms with local employees and not companies outsourcing services outside of the country to save money. Otherwise, while attempting to mitigate risk, you end up inheriting it. We have seen far too many corporate espionage and intellectual property theft cases involving cybercriminals posing as IT professionals. The work is often shared with employees in other countries, meaning you give passwords and accounts to one person and they share the credentials with a multitude of individuals that will "assist" with the work.

When you conduct penetration testing, you should be extremely cautious and make sure you understand exactly who is conducting the work and from what source IP addresses. The wrong people could steal your source code or worse, plant back doors in your systems so they can get paid by larger cybercrime groups to provide the "in" to your network. Unfortunately, this is often common practice in less developed countries, places where you have no recourse.

Risk Mitigation: Don't use offshore resources.

Due to the lack of highly skilled penetration testing professionals onshore, most large security services firms tend to look outside the borders to find assistance. This is great for the large firms because of their increased profit from the services and bad for you because you could fall victim to a real cybercriminal posing to be an ethical hacker. You may get your penetration test and also have remote access tools installed or critical data stolen from your business. Make sure that the professional testing your enterprise is in the United States or from another trusted country.

6. Risk: Customer Wants to Conduct Their Own Penetration Test

We have had a few clients that get requests from potential customers who want to conduct their own penetration test against the client's enterprise and service offering space, using their internal resources, before doing business with them. This is a bad idea for a few reasons and in most situations, you should never agree to these requests. You won't necessarily know who's doing the testing or what is being done. The outcome could mean that they back out of the deal based on the findings or hold you to fix everything that was found before they purchase services from you. Lack of professionalism and unknown resources testing your environment could leave you with more problems than you started out with.

Risk Mitigation: Use a 3rd party or already have the attestation in hand.

You can always ask the customer to pick a reputable 3rd party cyber security provider and at best, you share the service fee or build it into your pricing. Usually, if the customer is demanding a penetration test before solidifying any services, they have heavy compliance requirements when dealing with 3rd parties. Their intention is to use their internal penetration team as a way to get around costs. In a perfect world, this would not be a terrible idea if the team consisted of qualified individuals. You could get a free risk assessment and lose the deal at the same time. The idea is to never let any customer perform a penetration test against your technical resources, unless you are 100% certain they are prominent enough to have a seriously mature cybersecurity program, one that would contain purple team components and capabilities. Make sure they go over their protocol or methodology for penetration testing and that they have the monetary assets or insurance to cover any issues they may accidentally cause. If you ever go forward with such a request, you should also have a written agreement before any testing occurs. Realistically, the best resolve is to conduct the penetration testing before your customers begin to ask for it. This way you can provide them with an attestation letter demonstrating that proper penetration testing was done. This will always make the sales transaction smoother.

> *"One who allows a customer to conduct a pen test is like one who allows a blind friend to cut their hair before their wedding."*
> —Ancient InfoSec Proverb

WHAT A PENETRATION TEST SHOULD DELIVER TO YOU

The organization conducting the penetration test should provide a comprehensive report that includes evidence of any and all findings. The report should present the level of risk to the target systems and also provide the attack surfaces checked (e.g. privilege escalation on web applications and SSH key hijacking for servers/network devices). If you have already had a penetration test and your report did not contain these items, you probably paid for a penetration test and only received a vulnerability scan. The tester should include a high-level risk matrix in the report that has prioritized remediations, based on their criticality to your environment.

PENETRATION TESTING EXTRAS THAT ARE "NICE TO HAVE"

Make sure you ask the tester to contact you immediately if anything exploitable is identified because most will wait to share findings until their report is complete. Knowing about issues as they are found will allow you to be aware of any critical findings so you can be proactive and ready with resolves.

You shouldn't have to wait 14 days to discover that you have critical risks. A lot can happen in that two-week period if you have unpatched systems or weak authentication controls. One of the clients that engaged us for post-breach response work had deployed their server into a familiar online distributed computing platform and was compromised in a matter of three hours after going live.

Also make sure your tester is providing you with all networks and IP addresses that are being used as part of the testing against your systems. This is to help your technical teams understand what sources were involved in the event something goes down because of the authorized testing or some other reason.

It drives us crazy when 3rd parties get paid to present the true risk values to their clients. When they take the garbage that their scanner labeled "high risk," like XSS, and then harp on the client to make it a priority to fix this problem, before they even know if it's really a problem. When in reality, the "problem" they identified doesn't even have an exposed attack surface for XXS to work without authentication or present a real attacker any value in the first place. It is far too common these days for companies to hire newbie-level engineers to be penetration testers and they have no idea how web applications or attack modeling works, that is if they even know how to run scans. Then they pretend to sell risk assessments and penetration tests. Where were these companies on issues like the Slow Post Attack? Oh wait, they ignored it because the scanner said it was a low-risk vulnerability. Fake "pen testing companies" need to stop selling snake oil because it's hurting our Nation's organizations and economy.

WHAT CAN YOU EXPECT TO PAY FOR A PENETRATION TEST?

While we touched on this in an earlier chapter, we'll discuss pricing and considerations specific to assessments and testing. Pricing for penetration testing varies greatly based on scope, complexity, target type, approach type (white box/black box/grey box), timing (testing during business or off-hours), and more. A full enterprise cyber risk assessment may run from $25,000 to hundreds of thousands of dollars. A web application penetration test generally starts around $8,500 and goes into the tens of thousands, while a network penetration test may start around $10,000 and go to $100,000+ depending on many factors.

The cybersecurity industry is beginning to commoditize penetration tests, advertising "one size fits all" pricing, using low rates to attract business. These canned penetration tests meet the needs of companies simply looking to "check the box" for a client request or compliance requirements. However, a customized solution is far more effective for a true understanding of risk. A tailored test will generally cost about 10% to 30% more than a commoditized test, while providing far more value. Customized solutions will generally offer extra capabilities such as vulnerability remediation support, retests to validate successful remediation, dark web or open source intelligence (OSINT) research, and additional consulting services to improve security posture.

A good cybersecurity services firm will understand the specific needs of the engagement after a thorough scoping discussion and will tailor the test to meet the business requirements.

Selling a penetration test is not the same as selling a car wash. The Bronze, Silver, or Gold package does not apply.

FIFTY SHADES OF PEN TEST

If you are not familiar with the primary categories of penetration tests, we'll give you a quick overview of the differences. Penetration tests are typically categorized as "white box," "black box," or "grey box." The category generally refers to the level of information the tester is provided with, prior to starting the test. It is important to note that the definitions of white/black/grey box can vary depending on who you're talking to.

This Is Generally How the Testing Types Are Defined.

The white box penetration test will use an authorized account on your systems and the tester will have complete knowledge of the environment. The tester may be given multiple types of user credentials, network diagrams, application code base, and more, prior to commencement.

The black box penetration test will not use any predefined accounts and the tester will have little to no information except for the IP addresses or web application URLs, which define the scope of the test.

A grey box penetration test, of course, sits between white and black box. The tester has limited information which usually includes test user credentials so authenticated testing can be performed.

The white box network penetration test, using an authorized account to conduct the scanning and testing, is a bit of a wash. It makes the large assumption that the "attacker" is an internal employee, or has already compromised your systems, and has obtained access to an account on your network. While white box tests are still necessary to ascertain all areas of risk, they are not for every organization. Only those few organizations that have implemented a defense in depth security strategy will get real benefits from these tests. This is because if you are just starting out, odds are high that you have not implemented practices like zero trust or security frameworks, like CIS.

The outcome of the white box penetration test may indicate that you need to perform a lot of remediation work and some of it is going to require additional technologies, which means additional people and budget. Make sure you expect this ahead of any white box penetration testing.

When performing penetration testing for web applications, it makes perfect sense for the test to cover authentication bypass (e.g. grey box). If your web-application uses accounts to allow login and work, it may be a good idea to have someone make sure the roles cannot be elevated (e.g. user to admin) or enrollment steps bypassed. This is especially true for software as a service (SaaS) vendors with customers using their web application to conduct work they deem critical. If this is the case for you, then you certainly want a grey box penetration test for your web application.

Regardless of type of test required, most will start with a black box approach. This penetration test gives a more accurate review from the perspective of a cybercriminal scanning your technologies looking for weaknesses. These tend to be less expensive as they don't take as long as the white-box methods, and they may not require as much remediation. To gain the most thorough understanding of your attack surface, you would want to conduct both black and white box tests. If you are just starting out and your budget won't allow it, a black box provides great strategic insight into what you need to better protect your organization in the near term. If this is your way forward, ensure the black box focuses on your publicly exposed assets for initial strategic security benefits.

MANUAL VS. AUTOMATED PENETRATION TESTING METHODS

You may hear the terms "manual" and "automated" being thrown in with questions regarding the type of penetration test. Simply put, you need both for a true test but one approach is not better than the other. They serve entirely different purposes. For most of the testing work we do, typically 80% would be considered automated and 20% are manual. Ultimately, 100% of tests involve automation despite what the industry might lead people to believe. Anyone in the information technology sector not leveraging automation is betraying the very essence of technology and computing.

> *"The wise practitioner will not do manually what can be automated, only performing manual tasks which require great care and are worthy of the human touch."*
> —Ancient InfoSec Proverb

Sure, we can conduct your whole penetration test using "manual only methods," but make no mistake, we're still using a piece of software (automation). The difference is defined by what functions the software is capable of and we'll need several different software packages, each serving individual purposes. Think of it like this, when you need work done on your car or truck, like changing the brakes, this can be considered a manual task. Likewise, calling the dealership and having them drive a loaner car to your home, pick up your car and take it for services before returning it back to you could be considered an automated task. Sometimes you can accomplish the same result using a manual or automated method. Other times you are forced to use one or the other.

For a moment, let's focus on the actual task of changing brakes because someone must have the responsibility of conducting the work. If this is perceived to be a manual task, consider this: We could do most of the work to change brake shoes with a wrench set, as we'll need a few wrenches of various sizes. So, say we need 10 mm, 14 mm and 18 mm to get the brake calipers off and replace the brake pads. We are still using a tool, which is considered automation in the computing world, to perform this manual task. If the task was truly manual, we would be taking off the nuts and bolts with our fingers alone (human/manual power only). It would take a really long time and quite possibly cause the loss of fingers. Sounds silly to do it that way, right?

CYBER RISK ASSESSMENTS AND PENETRATION TESTING

Penetration testing and the review of electronic architecture are handled pretty much the same way. You have human expertise, combined with the right tools for the job. There is another form of automation for penetration testing, the black box (not to be confused with the black box approach to penetration testing). These are preconfigured devices that a vendor may have you install in your infrastructure. These boxes, once turned on, conduct a series of automated tests against your software and hardware. Once complete, the box is powered off, unplugged and returned to the vendor for analysis. This could be compared to having someone from the dealership coming to your house to get your truck and leaving you with the loaner while they go and change your brakes. Just like we need the mechanic at the dealership to do the actual work of changing the breaks, we will still need a human element with expertise to analyze the output of the black box or with the use of any specific software packages out in the trade.

Don't get caught up in the manual versus automated penetration test hype. The reality is, different tools accomplish different tasks and some take more manual effort than others. Focus on defining the testing objectives and a good penetration tester will use the appropriate tools for the job.

If someone is selling a "manual" penetration test, it is usually to inflate the price based on the time it takes to conduct the test. You may think you are getting a more thorough understanding of your risk posture by having someone doing a manual test, but essentially you are paying ten times more for the same information that you would get from a standard penetration test that leverages some forms of automation.

Let's look at this another way. Say we compare two service offerings for cybersecurity penetration testing, one is "manual" and one is "automated." The automated service includes the use of a cloud platform for vulnerability scanning of web applications and system software. The automated service also leverages the use of Metasploit Professional to proof of concept (POC) exploit capabilities and attack surface validations. This service conducts a penetration test on an average size client in 40 hours of testing using automated and manual methods (80/20). Using the same client and scope of work, but changing the tools to include a more manual approach, the same test will now take 250 hours. It seems the vendors will need to charge more for manual testing because they only have time to conduct so many per year, yet the outcome of the report will most likely contain very similar data.

DON'T FORGET ABOUT PHYSICAL PENETRATION TESTING

So, you've spent two million dollars on new cybersecurity technologies to protect your business. That's great! Hopefully, you have some configurations to protect against things like USB insertions. If you still allow thumb drives (USB sticks) on end-user systems and you don't have protection in place, you could be asking for a whole lot of trouble.

Inserting a thumb drive with test malware is part of a practitioner's cyber risk assessment toolkit. A good practitioner will not get caught and you may never even notice when they insert the USB drive. Maybe they will use a distraction, like an item drop, the *"I forgot something"* excuse, or perhaps just wait until someone steps out of the room for a second. It is impossible for people to monitor and comprehend everything that is happening at all times. This is why it is so important to conduct physical penetration testing.

This type of testing also measures how your security staff and employees will react to real-world scenarios. Training certificates for your security staff don't necessarily mean they will follow protocol or even remember the protocol when an incident arises. Conducting continuous training exercises will ensure a routine of good habits, which will help your physical security staff react more efficiently and provide better control of the situation when it is not a test.

PHYSICAL PENETRATION TESTING: GAMES AND THEORY

Methods to conduct a physical intrusion reaction and response test can vary greatly, depending on the hiring of a world-class security firm or a hack-job team. If you have not heard yet (and do look the article up on ArsTechnica.com), in September of 2019, employees of a security firm that was authorized to do physical penetration testing on a few Courthouses in Texas and Iowa were arrested. They were trying to sneak into a building at night, wearing all black and carrying black tactical backpacks. The employees were even charged with felonies and spent 12 hours in jail, despite their authorization letter that was signed by the Judicial arms of these State Governments. They were also each given a $100,000 bond and it was noted, at the time of arrest, one of the testers had a blood alcohol content of 0.05. A Dallas County attorney later reduced the charges and they were eventually dropped.

However, it is interesting to note that this mayhem occurred because the security company didn't have quality testers and didn't know how to properly structure the legal documentation for a physical penetration test. They also didn't ensure that all proper authorizations were received, and that methodologies were agreed upon with clear and concise project deliverables.

This example brings us to our first lesson: When gathering the requirements for a physical penetration test, make sure you thoroughly review the statement of work (SOW), other legal documentation, and professional capabilities of any firm you hire to conduct a physical penetration test. We will spend some time talking about our experience and recommendations regarding the murkiness surrounding physical penetration testing and the social engineering skills required to be successful at bringing value to the client.

We'll also share a few stories from personal experiences and fill you in on some key areas that should be on the SOW for any physical penetration testing activities that you are conducting, both internally or outsourced.

The Passion Begins at a Young Age!

It seems like a lot of kids that grew up in the 70's and 80's were prone to sneaking out. Those were the days before parents worried so much about kidnapping and other dangers. Co-author, Lauro Chavez, was a born escape artist which created a foundational skillset that still serves him today. Figuring out how to get out of his crib was one of his first memories of hacking physical security controls. His mom would put him down in his room for bedtime and while he didn't know what time it actually was, he knew he was not ready to sleep. He had cool toys and he certainly didn't want to wait until the next day to play. He had blankets and toys in his crib and one of those precious items was a very large Winnie the Pooh stuffed animal. When he says large, he means like 3 feet tall by a foot or better wide. Back then, of course, no one knew about Sudden Infant Death Syndrome (SIDS) and maybe it would be dangerous by today's standards. However, no Winnie the Pooh was going to snuff him out in the night; he actually found out this oversized stuffed animal was his key to escape.

His crib was certainly wood and had bars on all sides, he'd say it was *"bombproof,"* a normal design of the cold war era. He wasn't strong enough to hold himself on the bars yet and climb out, but he could hurl himself over the rail, only if he had a crash pad. The Pooh bear was the perfect tool for that job! It allowed him to have glorious and unchallenged access to temporarily unauthorized toys and even to the TV at any hour of the night. It took his mom at least ten times to finally catch on. OK, he's not actually sure on that because he couldn't count yet, but it seemed like a lot. She finally took the Pooh Bear away. No more crib escapes for now, but his childhood days were a great start for a penetration testing career!

MECHANICS OF PHYSICAL INTRUSION

Let's get down to brass tacks and talk about how to conduct a physical penetration test. To give you a deeper insight, we are going to put you in the shoes of the physical penetration tester as if you were the one testing security at a company's headquarters. Visualize yourself in each of these scenarios and consider how it would apply to your own organization or to others that you know.

Remember, this information is to get you in the right frame of mind because every penetration test is different. The most important skill is the ability to think on your feet, and reacting appropriately to whatever the situation throws at you.

When you are working on gathering or building requirements for a physical penetration test, these are some important areas of focus to include. Remember, social engineering is a critical component to every one of these testing activities. The abilities of the tester to utilize strong social engineering tactics will vary depending on the practitioner.

1. Entry Points

When you conduct access tests on entry points, you want to make sure that you come with the mindset of a cybercriminal that needs to get past this hurdle in order to continue gaining access to the electronics inside. One of the first controls you will need to get past as the physical intrusion tester will be the entry points of the building. You certainly want to check for lock picking, if that is a primary control method protecting the entry point, but make sure it is done during daylight hours and under the supervision of the head of physical security for the location that you are testing. Certainly not at night, dressed in all black, and carrying a backpack full of stuff you probably don't even need. We don't want to be the ones to ruin the ending, but traditional locks can be picked.

Magnetic style locks that release from the inside, based on motion, and unlock from the outside using an RFID badge, are very common. Sometimes, the exit mechanism will also require a badge swipe, but more often than not, it's a simple motion sensor connected for emergencies. We certainly want to focus on these entry points first. What we've found to be very successful in getting past these types of magnetic doors is to abuse the motion sensor for exiting. It is possible to construct a motion detection device by using a piece of cardboard, or plain white paper, with baling wire, maybe 6 feet long. By fixing the piece of cardboard to the end of the wire, we can slip the cardboard and wire under the doors, or sometimes between them, and once past the doors, wave it like a magic wand to trigger the motion sensor and unlock the doors. We've also had success unlocking a door by using a single piece of cardboard, about 12 inches by 12 inches, and sliding it hard under the door to trigger the motion sensor. This was achievable because the gap under the door, between the kick plate and the carpet, was ½ inch wide.

When you are testing an RFID badge-entry door that requires a swipe to enter and exit, you will want discover the frequency emitted by the reader and its corresponding cards and test the possibility to clone badges. Amazon offers several RFID frequency cloning devices for under $50. Those devices will only work on low frequency RFID badge systems and their complimentary cards. Unfortunately, we have found that most companies have no idea about the strengths and weaknesses of frequencies, so they are still using the cheapest products, which, coincidentally, are all on the low frequency that can easily be cloned. With those systems, a working access card can be made in seconds, providing that we have access to either an existing active functioning card or the reader itself (within 2 feet).

The easiest way to check the frequency of the badge system when you are at a client site is to take an existing badge and shining a flashlight through the card, from the back, so you can see the RFID antenna that is inside the card, through the plastic. If the shape is a circle, it is most certainly a low frequency card. If it is a circle inside a square or any other shape, it's using a higher frequency and the simple frequency cloners will not work. You can still clone the cards, but you will need a piece of machinery that is a bit more complicated and it will require you to assemble it as a kit and know some basic programming. This type of device should only be used for clients that require extra levels of protection.

2. Guard Stations

While guard stations may seem impenetrable because they have people there in uniform, this couldn't be further from the truth. Most often we get past the guard stations with little to no problem for a few reasons. The most common weakness that leads to a successful entry is that most companies don't have enough guards to watch the amount of activity during the busiest hours of the day, like opening, lunch and closing. Sometimes the corporate office will have multiple entry points and one or more of the entrances are not guarded by a human, requiring only an RFID badge to unlock. Most companies will assign many tasks for a few security guards to accomplish at a single corporate office location. Many of them are servicing visitor badges to guests and signing in contractors. Sometimes they may need to reconfigure an employee badge so this becomes their priority and, making things worse, their computer might be in a security office away from the main entry locations.

> *"The one who says 'I can gain access' and the one who says, 'I cannot gain access' are both correct."*
>
> —Ancient InfoSec Proverb

Anytime we're conducting a physical penetration test, we're conducting surveillance for at least a few hours, a few days prior to the launch. Usually we're sitting in a vehicle in the parking lot, listening to podcasts while watching the patrons and employees come and go. Lunch time is always great because many companies have large teams that like to take lunch together. It is even better when a company has a potluck or a similar gathering in a large conference room. However, landing on those is more luck than planning. Showing up just as the company is hosting a party is uncommon and most companies will ask to schedule testing around events.

Lunch is a vulnerable time at most places and it has offered the best results when trying to move past the guard stations. It is great because if you can park well and you can time your movement, you may be able to tailgate in with a large group returning to work from their local favorite taco spot and even better if they're running late for a meeting.

It's usually better to not use a fake badge which looks like a working badge, but that doesn't function at all. We find this to be a bad strategy for several reasons and it will get generally get you caught. Then you'll have to use that "get out of jail free" authorization letter sooner than you had anticipated. One key reason why using a fake badge is a bad idea is very simple. If there is a badge access door, the protocol is most likely for everyone to swipe to enter. Having a badge that doesn't work, because it's a fake, will get you sent straight to the security desk for interrogation and inspection of the badge. When everyone sees you swiping your fake badge like a clown, they are more likely to wonder if your access was restricted.

Saying you don't have a badge, for some made-up reason, is a much better option but it can also get you pinched. If you didn't do adequate research and can't state the names of people you "work with," pretending to be the new guy that doesn't have a badge or claiming you are there for an interview probably won't get you through. The one excuse that usually prevents questioning and gets us to tailgate past the mandated badge process is saying something like, *"I forgot my badge in the meeting room"* or *"I left it in my car."* This allows for a safe fail and offers the opportunity to try again a few moments later with a different crowd. The line, *"I forgot it at my desk because I'm not used to wearing one yet"* will usually get one of the employees in the lunch crowd to let us in.

Turnstiles or any other types of man trapping devices will unfortunately present quite a bit of a challenge. If you can't squeeze past one, jumping over will certainly get eyes drawn to your location. If being seen is your intent and you are onto aggressive entry for reaction and response testing, by all means, leap away and expect to be chased. Otherwise, try another entrance or wait to ensure the best timing.

There are a lot of physical security assessment amateurs out there who think by picking someone's office door lock, dressed in black military spec clothing, they are going to bring value. This is the equivalent of someone paying us because we can pick up a rock and break the glass window in their home.

3. OSINT for Company Required Attire

Preliminary Open Source Intelligence (OSINT) research and surveillance with special attention to company attire are extremely beneficial. When you're attempting to gain access to a building or facility, make sure you dress accordingly, especially if you plan to sneak past the guards. In the real world, if we want to get into a building and deploy some ransomware or a remote access toolkit using a Raspberry Pi, we are certainly not going to be dressed in all black, looking like idiots prying around at night. We're going to walk in during normal business times, dressed as one of the company's own personnel. Sometimes that's a business suit, to play the *"I'm late to a meeting and need to print this file"* consultant, or wearing specifically colored scrubs to play the lab technician. No matter what role you pick to play, make sure the business attire is something reviewed heavily as it will assist greatly in the passive entry and allow you to persist your activities during normal business. It's important to look the part and fit with the business culture at every location you are testing. That will be different at every company, so do your research.

> *"The wise one understands when on the Internet of Things, everything typed, posted, pasted, uploaded, downloaded, searched, looked up, checked out, replied to, forwarded, sent, subscribed to, memberships of, favorite groups, scrolled up, scrolled down, browsed, swiped, and most certainly liked, is recorded for all of eternity to be reviewed by the unrighteous at a later date."*
>
> —Ancient InfoSec Proverb

4. Employees & Workstations

When we're conducting these tests, we're not onsite to push our way through aggressively and install a thumb drive. We're there to observe the actions of people and the process they follow. We are also not there to install any real-world malware on their systems. A simple insertion of a blank and non-functional "dummy" thumb drive is more than enough for a proof of concept of the physical threat.

Deploying real malware to a company's network can result in litigation. We've heard stories of firms that were given access to full network and system data rights to conduct a penetration test who ended up steeling the data they were paid to research for weaknesses and risk. We can't emphasize this enough; know who you are hiring and their methodologies for conducting these tests.

Is it bad that we like to have extra fun testing employees on this subject? Once inside a facility, we like to identify vacated workstations so we can get quick access to the USB ports and take some evidence photos of the dummy thumb drive inserted. It is usually okay if the workstations are near other employees, as long as we act like we belong there. As the test progresses, we will focus on workstations that have employees present and stop by to ask if we can install some new software from our thumb drive onto their computer. When questioned, we always say we're a new hire from the information technology department, or similar department, matching the term the company uses. We're always smiling and being very friendly with our requests. Believe it or not, it's pretty rare that we find employees that will actually let us plug a thumb drive into their computer. They usually say, "*no way*" and begin to ask questions. What is quite interesting is that they rarely have any idea how to respond or report the situation. They don't know if they are supposed to call physical security, their manager, the police, or all of the above.

It's important that anyone conducting these tests focus on using the physical aspects of deploying malware onto the technologies. Part of the overall cyber risk assessment may include conducting internal systems and network testing that would mimic or simulate the capabilities of a human or advanced malware threat, once deployed via thumb drive or other methods. The physical part of the penetration test does not include that perspective of risk. Meaning that if we can physically move past entry points and security guards to find at least one computer where we can insert our dummy thumb drive, this is enough evidence that something is wrong with education in humans, protocol, security guard training, or all of the above. Always be extra nice to everyone you encounter. You may actually get permission to install that new software from your dummy thumb drive. If the organization has a validated hardware intrusion security profile for USB ports on all end point systems, well you may just want to skip this part.

5. Employee Common Areas

Once inside, try wandering around a bit before starting to ask employees if you can plug in our thumb drive. We enjoy this part and it feels like a bounty for the day gig penetration testing. You are in the building, past the guards, and everyone thinks you are just one of the employees. Time to wander around and see what you can find; what kind of fun is there to get into, that sort of stuff.

Walking around a few times will give you the understanding of the common areas, like conference rooms and break rooms, restrooms, maternity rooms, etc. You might carry a piece of caution tape just in case we need time in one of the restrooms or maternity rooms. Simply run the piece of caution tape across the door frame and go inside. Most people will generally assume it's getting cleaned and this will give you some time to adjust your mini camera, microphone or both. You can also take a small breather to make some notes on the progress or set up your Wi-Fi Pineapple for testing the wireless network.

Dropping into an empty conference room is only a good idea for a very small amount of time. Typically, conference rooms are booked back-to-back at companies we've worked for. They are usually empty for short periods of time only. Get in there and check for ports, get your evidence and get back out. You can always sit with your laptop and squat in the conference room, while you take some notes, but be prepared to be asked who you are if attendees arrive for the next meeting looking to grab a good seat early. Grab a break room or a meditation room. We find those to be the best locations to conduct other activities, like Wi-Fi or network testing, or for just taking notes. It's a bonus if you can also find an active network port.

6. Available Wi-Fi Networks

While this portion of the physical penetration test does include some electronic signal testing, it is included in this test due to the signal leakage at the physical locations that allows the risk to be materialized. This gives cybercriminals a great leverage to conduct snooping from the parking lot or even from inside the building, in one of the break, conference, or maternity rooms.

We like to use the Dwall module on a Wi-Fi Pineapple device. Along with other native tools in the device, it allows us to successfully intercept all Wi-Fi networks, either hidden or the ones broadcasting their SSID. It is possible to clone the corporate wireless network and deauthorize some of the clients (laptops or mobile devices) in range to have them reestablish connection to our Wi-Fi device, now cloning their corporate wireless network SSID. Once they are connected, we can use

Dwall and begin to intercept information, like potential hashes and keystrokes.

We find that the best way to run the Wi-Fi device of your choice is from a powered backpack or in a backpack with a small external battery. This way you don't look suspicious with a wireless device on the table in the break room next to a vending machine with powdered donuts. If the signal is strong or the offices are close enough to the parking areas, you may be able to conduct your activities from your vehicle. However, we usually find that many companies don't have any parking within several hundred feet from the building, making signals weaker and the ability for hosts to stay connected more difficult.

Make sure the firm you hire to conduct the physical penetration test has the capability to check your wireless signal leakage and will also assess the physical placement of your wireless access points.

7. Critical Areas

Make sure that you validate IT or technology areas. Catching an IT admin leaving his workstation unlocked, as you are wandering around with your dummy thumb drive, is quite the pot of gold but it is not very common. It's still something that needs to be a focus area during your physical penetration test.

We've tested quite a few server rooms and IT areas and we've only been able to gain complete unauthorized access to one. It was an onsite data center, a large server room, guarded by keypad in a badge access protected area of the business, dedicated to IT personnel only. Co-author, Lauro Chavez, was able to gain access to the restricted areas of the building by using social engineering techniques, including the right attire, boxes of donuts and some tailgating. Once inside the main building, he wandered around for a while until he found the IT area. It was in the middle of the building, guarded by badge access controls. Luckily for him, training about tailgating was still not heavily enforced at this site and the entrance to the IT area happened to be close to a restroom. He only needed to wait about three minutes before an IT engineer came back to the IT area from a restroom break. He acted like he was texting on his phone and waited for the person to open the door, slipping in right behind them. While they did give him the eyeball, they didn't stop or challenged him.

As usual, he conducted the exercise during lunch, in broad daylight. Most of the IT employees were still out eating, leaving him mostly free to roam around. Towards a corner in the back of the IT area, he found a small room with two doors, leading further into the data center where all the racks of glorious business essential hardware lived. It was guarded with a keypad combination lock. There were no other ways to get inside that didn't involve squeezing into the ventilation areas. However, he remembered seeing an employee working at a desk as he made his way into the IT area toward the data center. He began to go around to computers in the IT area, plugging in his dummy thumb drive and taking evidence captures with his micro camera. The employee didn't seem to notice him as he proceeded to insert the thumb drive in every engineer's computer he could find.

After a while, he thought he'd take a chance and ask the employee if they would let him into the data center. What did he have to lose? He had his evidence and it was time to move onto the part of this test where he'd get caught, in order to assess employee reactions to unauthorized activity. Having done some OSINT research prior, he knew the name of one of the principal network administrators that worked there. He walked up and very politely, excused himself to the employee for interrupting their work. After asking how their day was going, he told the employee that he was a contractor working in the onsite data center with a network administrator, making sure to drop his name. He said that the administrator was in there but he probably couldn't hear him knocking to get back in after going to the restroom. The employee smiled and walked me over to the door where they punched in the combination, right in front of him, and let him into the most safeguarded area in the whole company. Yes, he was just lucky but he most certainly plugged the thumb drive in the servers and took glorious evidence photos. Let us tell you, that made for an interesting presentation to the executive team!

You want to make sure that you are including critical areas in your physical penetration testing requirements. These are going to be places like onsite server rooms or data centers. You will also want to check for any IT closets, sometimes referred to as "telco closets" or "network closets." These are the small rooms that provide a hub-based extension to other parts of the office. They will usually include telephony equipment, like punch boards and tracks of data cables, leading to switches or possibly a firewall, with an available USB port. Some critical areas will also include the information technology (IT) area, where all of the company's IT engineers, architects, and helpdesk employees are working from. These are the individuals with the highest level of access to systems. If you can catch one of them making a mistake, like leaving a workstation unlocked with an admin shell running, then your victory meal will taste just a bit sweeter.

Maybe they have some tools on a thumb drive they left on their desk. You may also find drives or working RFID badges. Desk surfing a bit, if you can manage it, is not a bad idea. Sometimes, you will find installation disks with gold images and other interesting tools the teams are using to deploy and configure the technologies for the business. Though the tester should never open closed drawers, unless it's in the presence of the employee that owns it, items left on the desk are fair game when it comes to reporting evidence. You also shouldn't remove any items from the desk either. Use photos, instead, to demonstrate the evidence of the control violation that is causing risk. We never like to physically disturb any areas we're testing if we can manage. We will certainly plug the dummy thumb drive into a computer's USB port and get a photo for the report, but we will not disrupt anything else, if we can help it.

REACTION AND RESPONSE PROTOCOL CHECKS FOR YOUR STAFF

The steps taken by security guards and employees to ensure that a threat is identified and remediated is a critical aspect of physical security. Consider including the following criteria when testing for the reaction and response capabilities of your staff and physical security team:

1. Security Guard: Ensure to Empty the Suspect's Pockets.

The tester may have a backup thumb drive in their pocket. A security guard might take hold of the drive in the hand of the tester, or the one that was put in a computer, and then think the threat is resolved. Make sure your security staff knows to empty out pockets. We like to carry multiple thumb drives during assessments for this exact reason. More often than not, the security guard will never ask a tester to empty their pockets when detaining them as part of the exercise. We've even managed to drop a test malware file onto a security guard's own computer when they stepped out for a phone call. Sure, he was trapped and couldn't get out of the room, but he was left there with two computers, both had exposed USB ports, and his backup thumb drive was full of tools. Oh yeah, party time!

2. Security Guard: Leverage Two-party Control Over a Suspect.

You never know what someone is capable of. This is why it's always a good idea to maintain two-party control over any would-be criminal that walks into your office. Most of the time, when apprehended, we're escorted by a guard to the security office or to a conference room for containment. If we are not watched closely, we attempt to break away from the single guard with a hasty walk to see what secondary responses will look like. This is much more difficult when one guard remains in the same room while the other stands by the door or when they both escort us to the location where we are to be detained. Conduct training or send your security staff to expert law enforcement officer-type

CYBER RISK ASSESSMENTS AND PENETRATION TESTING

training to ensure they understand and practice the concepts of controlling suspects.

Once apprehended by a client's security staff at taser point, Lauro surrendered his authorization letter and asked them not to fire, explaining that he would comply without putting up any struggle. Upon hearing these words, the guard relaxed a bit and dropped his weapon to his side, eventually holstering it. This would have been a great opportunity for a real criminal to take advantage and overcome the security guard. Ensure that your security staff is trained to keep all suspects under control, with allowed weapons, at all times until they are assured the suspect can no longer be a threat.

3. Security Guard: Staff Appropriately.

Most of the time we're able to slip by the security desk to get further into the building. The reason we're successful is that there are usually too many people for one or sometimes even two guards to watch carefully. We will casually come into the waiting area and wait like we're supposed to be there for an interview or something (even ready to explain this, if asked by one of the guards). We will wait until a few visitors pop in for badges or see employees bringing in a vendor or food and then make a move. We're successful because there are not enough security guards to watch and monitor body language. Make sure to run test exercises to find out how many physical security staff you need to effectively protect your entrances. Also tests for high volume of service request times.

Companies will often use temporary security guards for certain tasks, like offboarding (terminating) a questionable IT administrator when management worries about the untrustworthy individual coming back to their desk. It happens. Anyway, it is common to see guards over the age of 60 in such a role, as the security guard business has largely become an industry populated with seniors. This is certainly not a problem for many, but depending on the type of company and the nature of the business, you may consider having appropriate backup.

If your visitor and badge functions require electronic input, you can expect some level of distraction to occur, giving opportunity for someone to sneak past a person who is legitimately signing in. Posting an extra guard to watch people coming in and out, without the distraction of any other functions, such as signing in visitors, might be a wise option.

4. Employee: Look for Visitor and Employee Badges.

Once we've gotten past the guard station, we're usually free to roam unchecked and unchallenged around the building. This is because the employees are not trained to be mindful of strangers without visitor badges. In fact, most won't even notice people without a badge of some kind. This is why training your staff is critical to being successful in the eventuality that someone with real malware on a thumb drive makes it into the building. We find that the most successful organizations use an incentive method when their employees call out security for incidents, like not wearing the proper badge or tailgating.

Remember, a visitor escort policy should be enforced, requiring all visitors to stay with their escort and not roam any areas on their own. Think of this like keeping your kids close when you bring them to the office. You never know what happened to that gum your daughter was chewing on when she's asking for another piece. She only left your side for a moment, yet she doesn't know where it went or is not admitting that she knows. We hope it is not on Clint's seat, keyboard, monitor, or desk. Perfect, it turns out she plugged the old gum in his USB port! We'll call it sticky security and make it the new policy to deter USB drives.

5. Employee: Identifying Suspicious Activity.

All of your employees need to receive training to identify suspicious activity. Typically, when we're onsite conducting one of these tests, we'll ask random employees questions, such as, *"Where is the IT Server room located?"* or *"Where is the CIO's office?"* and sometimes,

CYBER RISK ASSESSMENTS AND PENETRATION TESTING

"Where is your backup generator located?" Most of the time the employee will point in the general direction or smile and just say, *"I'm not sure."* Rarely will we find an employee to look us up and down and ask about why we don't have a visitor's badge, who we're here to see, or what happened to our escort.

There should be training that includes the signaling of issues, such as not wearing a visitor badge, or noticing an unknown person in the office. Training your employees to better understand the social engineering techniques of cybercriminals will help them identify that suspicious behavior in the office. The person digging outside in the trash next to the office... that is not normal and doing nothing is not the right answer. No, someone else won't take care of it and yes, it is each employee's responsibility to respond as per policy.

6. Employee: Reporting Protocol for Suspicious Activity and Other Violations.

One of the questions we always like to ask employees when we're conducting a physical penetration test is, *"Would you mind if I plug my thumb drive into your computer?"* We're always very nice when we ask. When they question why, we just say, *"I'm the new guy from IT and we are installing new software on all computers."* The interesting pattern that emerges when you do this over and over again is that while the employee may refuse to let you insert the thumb drive and know you're a phony, they almost never know what to do next. They simply think they have passed the test by refusing to allow the USB install only. Unfortunately, you must have that notification process to help people understand what actions come after they recognize the phony IT tester (or the truly malicious individual).

Just to help out the unsuspecting employee, we'll tell them that this is a test and "I need you to call physical security to let them know some random person is here attempting to install something from a thumb drive." Make sure your staff is aware of the appropriate protocol to follow, the number to call, and/or what email inbox to use to report suspicious activity, based on the situation.

We cannot overemphasis the importance of physical security which is why we took a deep dive into the testing process and considerations around securing your environment. Physical intrusion testing (or physical penetration testing) is an important component of a cyber risk management program, especially for organizations with large headquarters and multiple remote locations.

Think about it like this: Why would a cybercriminal spend tremendous resources trying to break through your external network defenses from the outside when they can simply hire someone in your city (or even an employee) for $500 on the dark web to show up at your office and plant malware on a computer that already has access to the internal network? It's a far greater reality than most realize.

WHAT THE CYBERCRIMINALS ARE UP TO (DARK CAMPAIGNS)

We know that you have probably heard a lot of information about implementing "cybersecurity control this" and "centralized logging that" and maybe even "at rest" encryption stuff. At some point you must have asked yourself, *"Why?"* Cybercriminals have been asymmetric enemies, much like we see in other types of conflicts, especially those associated with terrorism. Cybercriminals are essentially terrorists that operate primarily in a digital environment, as opposed to a physical one. Whatever you call the individuals and groups that are looking for ways to abuse technologies, it's important that you study the methods they are using to conduct their dark campaigns. The dark web is where many security researchers will focus their time but mainstream, and even underground news, rarely talks about it.

CYBER RISK ASSESSMENTS AND PENETRATION TESTING

There is more action going on behind the scenes on the Internet than in all Hollywood movies combined, but no one is talking about it. It is even estimated that Google indexes less than 5% of the content on the Internet.

Here are examples of dark campaigns that are active and ongoing today:

1. Op New-Up Screw-up

Continuous and unauthorized vulnerability scanning against known virtualized vendor in the IP space (Amazon AWS, Microsoft Azure, IBM SoftLayer, Rackspace, just assume all public subnets, etc.) is occurring around the clock. Cybercriminals are looking for attack surfaces on technologies, both new and existing. They are betting on your company using a new technology or feature up (new up) without the proper security testing (screw-up).

Cybercriminals are continuously scanning the IP spaces belonging to major vendors of distributed computing services. Installing services in the "cloud" may look good from a budget perspective but make sure that you are configuring all technologies securely and don't expect the vendor to do it for you. Unless you specifically pay for it, you are not going to get appropriate security. Even security controls like Web Application Firewalls and DDOS protection will cost extra. If you remember, we mentioned previously a client we've assisted, post-breach, after they installed a new technology on one of these cloud vendors' frameworks and it was compromised in less than three hours!

This is why. The moment anything new pops up, it is getting picked up by a scan within a day and the outcome is being reported back to cybercriminals. From here they take the next available steps, which will usually lead to a smash and grab or block and lock. What are those do you ask? Keep reading.

2. DarkOp Smash and Grab

Ongoing Brute Force Login Campaigns. It doesn't matter if you are using Office 365 or Google Corporate for email, you should be advised that cybercriminals are successfully taking advantage of email account leaks by using valid emails addresses and attempting many different password combinations until they find a successful one. Once they log in as you, they will lock you out, and possibly your whole company if you are the global admin of your Office 365 portal.

Your information might have been caught in the loot of a 3rd party breach. Maybe you approached the 3rd party with some questions about a service or you've registered for something, and that's how they got your email. When they got hacked, your email was part of the dataset taken. Make sure that every online login you have is enabled to support multi-factor authentication. One Time Passwords are best, using an authenticator app, like RSA, Symantec VIP or Google Authenticator. It's also still a great idea to print out backup codes to keep in your physical floor safe. Once an attacker is able to get access to a global admin account, the whole organization is in for a wild ride.

3. DarkOp Block and Lock

Ongoing Ransomware Campaigns. We've recently seen some really dirty phishing campaigns being used to deliver ransomware. Cybercriminals use disaster situations with widespread issues, like the pandemic, to take advantage of frightened people not paying attention. We have seen emails, disguised to be from the World Health Organization, presenting a link to "updated spread data" that either sends people to a fake Google or Office 365 sign-in page, or it is asking them to accept the download, while the ransomware is disguised as an add-on.

Don't take ransomware lightly! We recently did a forensic investigation and incident management for an advanced Emotet variant breach which was using the locker virus set of tools to lock all files on computers and network drives. Nearly 2,000 devices were locked and rendered ineffective in a 48-hour period. One of the critical systems was a SQL database that held all the master files for the company's customers. This happened right in the middle of a pay week and it took the organization over a week to return to sufficient operation level and over a month for normal operations. Even with the assistance of the FBI, there were no options to unlock the files, other than paying the ransom.

Because the organization did not want to pay the multimillion dollars asked (in bitcoin), they opted to rebuild from snapshots taken over a week prior to the first logging notification of a breach. They thought Windows Defender would save them and never made any real backups of any critical data. They also were not watching logs or security alerts, largely because they didn't have a security team, or any IT professionals dedicated to the task. The availability of the snapshots was fortunate. Otherwise it would have far more time to bring the business back to normal. Based on our investigation, it appeared that the situation was all caused by an employee in the sales department who fell for a phishing email offering a gift card. This error led to the crypto-locking of millions of corporate files on local computers, servers, and shared drives.

The moral of the story is, don't get hit with ransomware. It is many, many times cheaper to prevent an attack than to remediate one.

VULNERABILITY VALIDATION AND RE-RANKING STRATEGY

Authenticated vulnerability scanning is the Hoover Dam flood method of understanding security misconfigurations. Remember that! If you have begun scanning for vulnerabilities externally and internally, with or without authentication, you may have discovered how many software misconfigurations are actually out there.

Windows will have updates every month. Other software will update as much as twice per month or more, depending on bugs, bounty or critical resolves that were found and which need to be addressed by patching. Some environments are going to be lean and patching will be as easy as turning on automatic updates for everyone and using the automated schedules to update your employee base. Others, however, have complex environments that include everything hosted onsite, from web applications, to the Microsoft Exchange Server, and clusters of SQL databases, not to mention the firewalls, network load balancers, and that web filtering product they were talked into installing.

You may be in a position of thinking that you'll never be able to catch up on vulnerability remediation but you don't need to worry about every vulnerability or misconfiguration out there right now. For the time being, you only need to worry about the critical ones that impact your specific architecture and deployment configurations.

As an example, maybe your web application was found to have a reflected cross site scripting vulnerability associated with the user's portal attributes. This sounds serious and the web scanner or tester may classify this as a high or critical item. Before you start making any budget changes or project scheduled modifications, take a look at potential ways to exploit what is being seen. In other words, seek to understand how a cybercriminal could exploit the vulnerability to put leverage on your business integrity.

In the example of the, would-be critical, reflected cross site scripting vulnerability that was found on 40 of your web applications, you may actually need to script cross site in order for your application to function. Also, if the vulnerability was identified after authentication, in the user's personalized container profile, and the type of customers you typically have in your web apps are large organizations that are paying for business services and functions, maybe it's a stretch to label this is a critical issue that needs to be resolved. In fact, many vulnerabilities should be re-ranked based on their exploitable probability, which will be based on your personalized architecture.

CYBER RISK ASSESSMENTS AND PENETRATION TESTING

It drives us crazy when a security tool labels a vulnerability as "critical" and companies get all spun up to resolve something that would only present a critical risk in the perfect architectural placement, like out in the DMZ and public facing.

Many vulnerabilities require the right conditions to be used in a truly malicious way. Vulnerability ranking is done based on a few factors, one of them being how severe the outcome could be. An example would be remote code execution or denial of service. If you use a technology on the public facing infrastructure and it contains a vulnerability that allows remote code execution, this could be serious. An investigation into a site, like Exploit DB, would show if there were any commonly used or proof of concept-based exploits for the RCE vulnerability. If working exploits are identified, this then becomes a quite serious situation and you are lucky that no one has found it to take advantage of it yet. Now that you know about this issue, fix it immediately. In all seriousness, this does occur more often than you think. Take the same RCE vulnerability and place it behind three firewalls, strong networking and your internal network controls, and the severity becomes significantly less. The placement of the technology within your architecture that has the RCE vulnerability and the ability for a cybercriminal to actually exploit it makes huge difference.

Whoever says, *"what about rogue admins?,"* is clearly drunk. If an admin wants to go rogue and become a disgruntled employee, then they certainly don't need to download and install penetration testing software, load up the RCE vulnerability exploit payload and execute it to get into your systems. They are admins! They can just log in and do whatever they please. They keep all your technologies running and if they wanted to do something mischievous, it could be as easy as copy-paste or shift-delete. They certainly don't need to install Metasploit or any other software to take advantage of the systems. Know who you hire... Period. If you hire a faulty admin, that's your fault, no pun intended.

The important thing to consider here is that if you are short staffed and the team you have is focused on other duties, having them patch several thousand vulnerabilities may not be something that you can take on, especially with new ones coming out so frequently. Vulnerability validation and re-ranking can help solve this problem by allowing the critical and noncritical ones to be weighed against the currently deployed architecture. If the conditions are not present to make the vulnerability exploitable or high-risk, then the criticality can be reduced and put into a more normalized patching sequence. This will give time for any additional testing or SME reviews and not make you think you need to resolve immediately, stressing all angles of your business because you're worried about getting hacked.

One way to validate whether the conditions exist or not is to use a tool like Metasploit to test any exploitable payloads identified for specific critical vulnerabilities. If the attack is not successful because the conditions for the exploit to work cannot be met, due to current architecture configurations and possible security configurations, then the "critical" ranking can now be reduced to "medium" and rolled into a normal patching schedule. Having cyclical penetration testing processes inserted into your change management processes is a great way to validate vulnerabilities and re-rank them.

ADVANTAGES AND DISADVANTAGES OF SIEM

Security Information and Event Management or (SIEM) is the process and technology that provides log analysis and review for your entire technology footprint. You may notice that PCI and CIS controls also require centralized logging and SIEM functions to be compliant, but what are we really dealing with here? Let us shed some light about SIEM systems, which they don't tell you during the sales process.

At one time, it was a coveted hacker move to gain unauthorized remote access to search and extract juicy data, and then clear the log

CYBER RISK ASSESSMENTS AND PENETRATION TESTING

files to destroy traces of activities, all before logging out with the loot. The electronic sleuth would then move in to determine what IP the hacker came in from and what files were taken out. They could potentially identify the individual that took the files and turn that address over to authorities, assuming the hacker didn't delete the log files.

We still tend to turn over IP data to the authorities, even when we know the road may lead to nowhere, but a lot has changed. When deleting log files was an opportune strategy for cybercriminals, operating systems were not as secure out of the box as they are today. Centralized logging has been a major security requirement for many years now and there are measures to prevent the clearing of log files, but cybercriminals have found a way to ensure that logs won't matter. Virtual Private Networking services have sprung up in mass in recent years. This provides an opportunity for bad guys to better mask their locations and activities.

Sure, your electron sleuth will still find some logs regarding when the breach occurred, what accounts and services were used, but the source IP can never bring certainty due to the massive benefits of VPN services and darknet nodes. They can easily log into Tor and then hit another external VPN server. It's simple, they might have those AWS servers they've compromised recently, they'll install a VPN client on one of them. This will provide good cover to drop a file locking malware on an unsuspecting business and ask them for a few bitcoins to get their systems unlocked.

Yes, there are still some benefits to logging all things centrally and having automation and human eyes on the prowl for suspicious activities. For one, in perfect form, this process of having a whole team of people who are actively looking at all parsed log data for indicators of compromise and anomalies alike is the most mature state of any aspiring cybersecurity program. However, many will never make it or even come close to this state. Those who adopt this process as part of daily operations may find that their sleuths seem to be chasing down ghosts rather than finding real cybercriminal activity.

The most famous chase is the brute force false alarm that always occurs when an employee is prompted to change their network password but forgets to update their mobile devices with the new password. When they see those "failed login attempt" log entries begin to pour into the SIEM dashboard, all the SOC team and incident responders get their palms sweaty and the trigger ready. This becomes a pain-in-the-rear reminder that the help desk team needs to handle more user-level training. Meanwhile, you're pissed off that Gerry forgot to change his password on his mobile devices again!

> *"The poor user of technology sharpens the sword of the one who manages it."*
> —Ancient InfoSec Proverb

Streamlining processes and resolving technology interconnectivity issues are some of the more common benefits of SIEM these days. Yes, it's there if you get breached, or if you are lucky, as the breach is actively taking place, but on most days, it will be creating tickets to stop the chatter of other internal tech communication issues. Besides, if your host-based controls fail and you get all the files in your network and systems locked by a crypto-ransomware, you may be glad that you had all the logs written off to a central location. You might also find that it didn't make much of a difference either way.

The logs will tell you, "The cybercriminal came from this IP address... at 4:20 p.m. and took the database file by putting it in a tar ball, then uploaded it to a server in Europe." Great, all the centralized logging in the world won't fix a misconfiguration that has nothing to do with logging and it won't get your data back either!

Be aware of a few important points when you decide to take on the SIEM requirement for your business. While this does provide an extra layer in the defense in depth strategy, it's not for the faint of heart or budget. Adopting this is costly and the process adds a heavy load to the daily operations.

First, understand what it takes to get a SIEM process 100% mature. Most importantly, you will need to aggregate or transport logs from each of your devices (e.g. laptops, servers, network devices, databases, web applications, etc.) to a centralized location, where your SIEM can then begin monitoring for suspicious issues, or suspected malicious events, like multiple logon failures with an incorrect password. You can certainly opt to go with a third-party service for SIEM if you don't feel it's something you can take on without budgetary means and even maybe human expertise needs.

Third-party services can certainly take some of the financial load off but what you might not realize is that you are now shipping 100% of your technologies' sensitive information to a provider outside of your control. You must now account for the risk of that third party getting breached. Is your data in the same system, virtual or not, with other tenants (multi-tenant environment)? How do they guarantee that your sensitive internal data is safe? There could be passwords and account names present in some of the logs that your technologies are sending. It would be a terrible thing for an employee of the third-party company to go rogue and attempt to sell this data to criminals on the dark web. Just keep this in mind when you are choosing between an on-premise and a third party hosted solution.

Here are a few items to be aware of if you choose to build the solution yourself, in-house and on premises:

1. Initial and annual costs for SIEM technology.
2. Complexity of log aggregation to the SIEM system.
3. Human expertise to manage and tune the SIEM technology.
4. Technology requirements and costs for log storage and retention.
5. Human workforce necessary to create tickets and investigate alerts produced by SIEM.

These are some considerations when deciding to go with a third party SIEM provider:

1. Does the provider's security compliance attestations, like the SOC which validates the third-party systems, implement the same rigor of security that they claim to sell?
2. What transport security is the provider using for logs in transit?
3. Architecture behind the compartment security at the hosting site to ensure log security.
4. Location of the data centers—U.S.A. or somewhere else?
5. The method to return or destroy log data upon contract termination.
6. Method used by the provider to verify the trustworthiness of its employees.
7. Your ability to handle the downstream effect of SIEM.
8. Human workforce necessary to create tickets and investigate SIEM alerts.
9. The initial and annual costs.
10. Cost of adding new devices or technology that you may purchase in the future.

CYBERSECURITY COMPLIANCE & FRAMEWORKS

Compliance is a daunting task and thorn-in-the-side for many. Yet, we can say with certainty that cybersecurity compliance requirements are here to stay.

In this chapter we will shed light on the subject of compliance and provide guidance to make your life easier. This is coming from years of experience and figuring it out the hard way. It will provide insights, whether you've been responsible for compliance for many years, or if you are facing it for the first time. We will explain the difference between frameworks and compliance requirements, provide an overview of the common standards in today's environment, and dive into a deeper discussion about how to build compliance into your organization's ongoing operations.

> *"The only guarantees in life are death, taxes, and compliance requirements."*
>
> —Ancient Infosec Proverb

While it is easy to feel overwhelmed with compliance requirements changing constantly, there is light at the end of the tunnel. Over time you'll realize that many regulations are simply stating the same requirements in different ways. The more frameworks you review, the more overlap you will recognize.

CYBERSECURITY FRAMEWORKS VS. CYBERSECURITY COMPLIANCE

Cybersecurity frameworks and cybersecurity compliance standards have a tremendous amount of similarity in how they describe the principles of cyber risk management. However, there are some key factors that make cybersecurity frameworks different from compliance standards. For example, frameworks guide what a company should do and have in place, from a holistic and enterprise-wide point of view. Frameworks also allow room for discretion and flexibility.

Meanwhile, cybersecurity compliance dictates the specific controls and standards that must be followed. Compliance is often industry specific or pertains to a specific type of data. For example, HIPAA compliance requirements apply primarily to the healthcare industry and the safeguarding of Protected Health Information or "PHI."

> *"He who is compliant may not be secure.*
> *He who is secure is likely compliant."*
>
> —Ancient Infosec Proverb

While aligning to a cybersecurity framework is optional for many organizations, whereas compliance is generally dictated, we always recommend that a company select and use an industry-recognized framework. Frameworks such as CIS Controls or NIST CSF act as a guide and a foundational set of proven best practices that are recommended by independent groups of security professionals. Cybersecurity frameworks allow a company to show that it is following an industry approved standard rather than making up their security program with an ad hoc approach.

Unfortunately, with a lack of proper guidance, most organizations start trying to achieve individual compliance requirements, without focusing on alignment to a standard cybersecurity framework. We call this the "whack-a-mole" approach to cybersecurity. When one requirement comes up, you focus time and resources on it and immediately another one pops up. This becomes a rat race of complexity and a major waste of resources, especially for fast-growing companies.

It is important for any organization, regardless of size, to focus first on aligning to a security framework. Most will find that once their organization is aligned to a framework, the vast majority of compliance standards are covered, even when faced with new requirements. In specific cases, a compliance requirement may also serve as a cybersecurity framework and vice versa.

> *"He who tries to kill a swarm of bees with a sling shot also chases many compliance standards without aligning to a framework."*
> —Ancient Infosec Proverb

The following section contains an overview of the common cybersecurity frameworks and compliance requirements. Please understand that this is not an exhaustive list. There are many more niche requirements designed for specific industries and applications.

It is also important to know that cybersecurity frameworks and compliance requirements change regularly. Therefore, these descriptions serve as a broad overview only. Individuals responsible for cybersecurity and compliance should review the official documentation for any framework or compliance requirement, which is provided by the appropriate governing body.

COMMON FRAMEWORKS

CIS Controls

Full Name: Center for Internet Security Critical Security Controls.

For Use By: Ideal for emerging and mid-market organizations not required to align with other frameworks.

Scope/Area of Focus: Enterprise-wide controls.

Audits: None required.

The CIS Controls framework is a set of 20 control categories that are meant to guide a wide range of organizations toward a strong cybersecurity posture. These controls are broken down into 3 implementation groups, referred to as, "Basic, Foundational, and Organizational." Each group is designed for companies of a different size and set of internal capabilities, ranging from small businesses to large enterprises. The CIS Controls framework is an excellent choice for many mid-market and emerging companies. It is simpler to implement than frameworks such as NIST SP 800-53 and ISO 27001, while being robust enough to define the appropriate security measures for the majority of companies in the United States.

NIST CSF

Full Name: National Institute of Standards and Technology Cybersecurity Framework.

For Use By: Intended to support the critical infrastructure systems that most production systems rely on, but broadly applicable for cyber risk management at organizations of all sizes.

Scope/Area of Focus: Enterprise-wide controls.

Audits: None required but may be requested by a customer.

The NIST CSF was published in 2014 in response to Presidential Executive Order 13636 which called for a standardized security framework for critical infrastructure organizations in the U.S. It leverages 5 standards/guides that together provide a comprehensive platform for cybersecurity operations, risk management, and strategic management. Moreover, NIST CSF is organized into 5 core functions that work in a symbiotic process to represent a secure lifecycle. The 5 functions are Identify, Protect, Detect, Respond, and Recover. Each of these core functions is essential to a sturdy security posture and the effective management of cybersecurity risk. The NIST CSF is a great guideline because it transforms organizational security from a reactive to a proactive approach. NIST CSF plays a central role in other frameworks, like Baldrige Cybersecurity Excellence Builder (BCEB), and the widely applied Cybersecurity Capability Maturity Model (C2M2), because it fills the gap between cybersecurity operations and risk planning efforts that are typically done at the executive level.

NIST SP 800-171

Full Name: National Institute of Standards Special Publication 800-171 (or 800-171a—where "a" indicates the revision).

For Use By: Ideal for emerging and mid-market organizations, especially those doing business with the U.S. Department of Defense handling Controlled Unclassified Information (CUI).

Scope/Area of Focus: Enterprise-wide controls.

Audits: None required.

NIST SP 800-171a is a recognized and respected cybersecurity framework that is appropriate for many mid-market and emerging companies. It was mandated for government contractors or organizations that handle sensitive U.S. Government data. It adheres to reasonably expected security requirements and is used to verify compliance with Defense Federal Acquisition Regulation Supplement (DFARS). Sensitive, but unclassified information, can include financial data, trade secrets, patents, and other items of national defense interest. There are 14 control categories that make up NIST SP 800-171a. These are Access Control, Awareness and Training, Audit and Accountability, Configuration Management, Identification and Authentication, Incident Response, Maintenance, Media Protection, Physical Protection,

Personnel Security, Risk Assessment, Security Assessment, System and Communications Protection, and System and Information Integrity. The NIST framework requires that organizations ask questions such as who is accessing what data, who can view what data, and if a breach occurs what plan do we have and who will be notified?

NIST SP 800-53

Full Name: National Institute of Standards Special Publication 800-53.

For Use By: Required for DoD prime contractors who operate federal information systems on behalf of the U.S. government. It is also beneficial for large enterprises with in-house IT and security departments, looking for a robust framework.

Scope/Area of Focus: Enterprise-wide controls.

Audits: Self-attestation is typically required for DoD contractors who are directly connecting to DoD networks, servers, or other systems.

The National Institute of Standards and Technology (NIST) has developed the initial version of the NIST SP 800-53 cybersecurity framework in 2006, with the intention to improve the security of the Federal Government. While it is not a requirement for most private organizations to follow NIST SP 800-53, it is a respected and recognized framework that is robust enough for adoption by large enterprises. It also helps organizations comply with the Federal Information Security Management Act (FISMA) which was designed to keep government agencies safe from cybersecurity threats. The framework is broken into 18 different families. These are Access Control, Audit and Accountability, Awareness and Training, Configuration Management, Contingency Planning, Identification and Authentication, Incident Response, Maintenance, Media Protection, Personnel Security, Physical and Environmental Protection, Planning, Program Management, Risk Assessment, Security Assessment and Authorization, System and Communications Protection, System and

CYBERSECURITY COMPLIANCE & FRAMEWORKS

Information Integrity, System and Services Acquisition. NIST SP 800-53 is very detailed and can be a great framework to strengthen the security of an organization. However, it is generally used by Federal Government suppliers and large enterprises. NIST SP 800-53 is not always the best option for mid-market and emerging companies.

HITRUST CSF

Full Name: Health Information Trust Alliance Common Security Framework.

For Use By: Used primary by healthcare organizations handling any type of Protected Health Information (PHI).

Scope/Area of Focus: All systems with direct or indirect access that could lead to compromise of PHI, to include digital and physical assets (e.g. printed documentation).

Audits: Organizations may follow HITRUST without audits. However, formal audits should be performed by an authorized HITRUST assessor if the goal is to demonstrate HITRUST Certification.

HITRUST CSF is among the most widely adopted security frameworks in the U.S. It was created by IT and healthcare professionals to create an efficient framework for managing security requirements that are common in the healthcare industry. One way HITRUST differs from HIPAA is that HITRUST is a framework whereas HIPAA is a federal law. HITRUST certification is a rigorous security evaluation that is often used to demonstrate compliance with standards, such as HIPAA and ISO/IEC 27000-series. The framework addresses security, privacy and regulatory challenges that many healthcare organizations face. Moreover, it takes a risk and compliance-based approach so that organizations can tailor their security controls based on their specific size, systems, and regulatory requirements.

ISO 27001

Full Name: International Organization for Standardization 27001.

For Use By: Ideal for large enterprise doing international business with in-house IT and security departments.

Scope/Area of Focus: Enterprise-wide controls.

Audits: Formal certification requires audits performed by an accredited 3rd Party Auditor.

ISO 27001 is a framework that is internationally recognized. It consists of standards developed by the International Organization for Standardization and the International Electrotechnical Commission, which are defined in 14 control categories. These include Information security policies, organization of information security, human resource security, asset management, access control, cryptography, physical and environmental security, operations security, communications security, system acquisition, development and maintenance, supplier relationships, information security incident management, information security aspects of business continuity management, and compliance. This framework can be used to manage medium to large companies and can be used in multiple industries, such as finance, telecom, and IT companies.

ISO 27002

Full Name: International Organization for Standardization 27002.

For Use By: Ideal for large enterprise, doing international business, with in-house IT and an established, mature information security program.

Scope/Area of Focus: Enterprise-wide controls.

Audits: Formal certification requires audits performed by an accredited 3rd party auditor.

ISO 27002 is supplementary to ISO 27001, meaning to use ISO 27002, the organization must have already adopted the ISO 27001 framework. The biggest difference between the two frameworks is the amount of detail they provide and the application of controls. ISO 27002 goes into a deeper level of detail about each control and what is needed for compliance. This framework is geared towards very large companies that already have a strong grasp on the ISO 27001 framework and that have the resources to carry out a very strict and detailed control schema.

COBIT

Full Name: Control Objectives for Information and Related Technologies.

For Use By: Ideal for large enterprise with in-house IT and security departments. It is commonly used by organizations that need to comply with SOX, as well as organizations who need to maximize the value of IT-related investments. These companies usually depend on technology for reliable information.

Scope/Area of Focus: Enterprise-wide controls.

Audits: There is no formal independent audit requirement.

COBIT is generally regarded as an audit framework that provides a common language for IT staff, executives, and compliance auditors to communicate about IT controls. Without a common language, an enterprise being audited has to repeatedly educate auditors about when, why, and how their IT controls were enacted.

This framework was created by the Information Systems Audit and Control Association (ISACA). It is an IT governance framework that helps managers bridge the gap between control requirements, technical issues, and business risks. COBIT can be used not only as a planning tool for information security, but also as a control model as it provides advice on the implementation of sound controls and control objectives.

ISACA incorporates five principles in COBIT that focus on the governance and management of IT within an organization. These principles are to meet stakeholders' needs, cover the enterprise end-to-end, apply a single integrated framework, enable a holistic approach, and separate governance from management. COBIT is the only business framework for the governance and management of enterprise IT. Despite COBIT being initially designed as an IT governance and management document, it includes a framework to support information security requirements and assessment needs. Moreover, COBIT enables organizations to sustain continuous risk management operations and helps them better prepare for information security risk operations.

COMMON COMPLIANCE STANDARDS

PCI-DSS

Full Name: Payment Card Industry Data Security Standard.

For Use By: Organizations handling credit card data or dealing with credit card transactions, even those using 3rd party systems for processing.

Scope/Area of Focus: Any infrastructure communicating with devices processing or storing credit card data.

Audits: Certification requirements will vary. It is the volume of credit card transactions that determines the level of PCI compliance required. Requirements range from self-assessment questionnaires to formal 3rd party audits by an accredited PCI Qualified Security Assessor (QSA).

The Payment Card Industry Data Security Standard (PCI-DSS) is required for all vendors handling credit card payment transactions. Enforcement is generally conducted by merchant banks. PCI is broken down into 4 levels, with each one based on the annual volume of credit card transactions processed. Level 1 merchants process over 6 million cards annually, whereas Level 4 merchants process fewer than 1 million

CYBERSECURITY COMPLIANCE & FRAMEWORKS

in total, with less than 20,000 via e-Commerce. Regardless of the merchant level, PCI contains 12 overlapping control categories that need to be in place. These include the requirement for a firewall to be configured and installed, change of default passwords on all technologies, protection of cardholder data, encrypted transmission of cardholder data, up-to-date anti-virus software, application security and maintenance, cardholder data must be on a need-to-know basis, every person with computer access must be given an ID, physical access to the cardholder data must be restricted, all cardholder data and network resources must be tracked, security systems must be tested regularly, and policy dealing with information security must be reviewed and maintained. The complexity of these controls will vary depending on the organization's merchant level.

HIPAA

Full Name: Health Insurance Portability and Accountability Act.

For Use By: Used primary by the healthcare industry and organizations handling Protected Health Information (PHI).

Scope/Area of Focus: All systems with direct or indirect access that could lead to compromise of PHI. It includes digital and physical assets (e.g. printed documentation).

Audits: Audits tend to be performed internally, or by 3rd parties for internal use. Most proactive organizations conduct internal audits as a best practice but they are not held to a 3rd party audit requirement. An organization may be forced to have an independent audit if the violation of patient privacy is reported.

The Health Insurance Portability & Accountability Act (HIPAA) is a standard that all organizations handling Protected Health Information (PHI) need to follow. This includes hospitals, health insurance companies, clinics, and others who handle patient information. Cybersecurity is one major aspect of HIPAA. According to HIPAA's cybersecurity guidelines, the general requirements for compliance are to ensure the confidentiality, integrity, and accessibility of all electronic PHI, to identify and protect against likely threats, to protect against likely data disclosure or leakages, and to ensure compliance by their employees through policy and training.

FINRA

Full Name: Financial Industry Regulatory Authority.

For Use By: Financial institutions within the investment industry.

Scope/Area of Focus: All systems with direct or indirect access that could lead to the compromise of financial information and communications. It includes digital and physical assets (e.g. printed documentation).

Audits: FINRA operates on appointment by the SEC to enforce securities regulations and to verify that an organization's financial filings match reality. Audits are performed by FINRA and initiated when they send a notice to an organization. If no violations are found, the exam is complete. But, if the auditor finds exceptions, the firm must provide FINRA with a written response that is addressing the corrective actions that the organization plans to execute.

FINRA is a compliance standard that protects investors and it oversees U.S. broker-dealers. That means banks, investors, and certain financial applications must meet this compliance. FINRA expands beyond cybersecurity. For example, it requires financial services companies to keep records of all communications for a period of 7 years. In terms of cybersecurity, FINRA's overall goals are to identify threats, protect assets, and have a disaster recovery plan for the eventually of a breach occurring or if data is lost. In practice, this includes having strong technical controls, testing incident response plans, researching vendors to prevent supply chain attacks, training staff, and sharing intelligence with other organizations.

CMMC

Full Name: Cybersecurity Maturity Model Certification.

For Use By: All organizations functioning within the supply chain of the U.S. Department of Defense.

Scope/Area of Focus: Enterprise-wide controls.

Audits: An annual 3rd party audit is required by an authorized CMMC auditor.

The Cybersecurity Maturity Model Certification (CMMC) is a requirement for all contractors that work with the DoD, as of January 2020. Third party auditors have been applying for accreditation from the CMMC Accreditation Body since early 2020. Details on how the assessments will be conducted are anticipated soon. The CMMC AB plans to establish a CMMC Marketplace that will include a list of approved assessment organizations. DoD contractors must learn and prepare for the CMMC technical certification requirements as it is important for long-term cybersecurity agility.

CMMC ties in with the NIST framework and others, but it contains five maturity levels. Each contractor will have to meet a specific level based on their size, industry, sensitivity of information, and criticality to the Department of Defense (DoD) supply chain. The higher the level, the stricter guidelines the company needs to follow. At Level 1, only 17 controls need to be met. For the most part, these controls are based on cyber hygiene, having solid documentation, limiting physical security, and having anti-virus installed. Level 5 is the most complicated, with a total of 171 controls, which would be considered advanced and progressive in their implementation. The CMMC model is now considered the unified standard for DoD acquisitions, replacing the previously required, but rarely enforced, NIST SP 800-171a.

SOC 2

Full Name: System and Organization Controls 2.

For Use By: Organizations providing a system or service automation, primarily with a business to business (B2B) focus.

Scope/Area of Focus: Implementation and sustainment of security controls within the system that is being provided as a service to companies.

Audits: Annual formal examination by an accredited accounting firm under the American Institute of Certified Public Accountant (AICPA) system examination guidelines.

SOC 2 was created for service providers that store customer information. It is common for SaaS companies and also includes MSPs, ISP, MSSPs, and ASPs. SOC 2 requirements include a total of 5 primary criteria that all applicable organizations must follow. This criterion includes Privacy, Security, Availability, Processing, and Confidentiality. Specifically, SOC 2 requires that the company sets up alerts on particular events. In order to be compliant, the alerts must be triggered for data exposure or modification, file transfer activities, and account activity.

There are 2 types of SOC reports. A Type I exam looks at the description or design of controls as of a specified date. In a Type I report, there is no further testing beyond the specified date. A Type II report contains control descriptions in addition to following up on each control's effectiveness over a period of time. This period of time typically covers 6 to 12 months after commencement of the examination.

SOC for Cybersecurity

Full Name: System and Organization Controls for Cybersecurity.

CYBERSECURITY COMPLIANCE & FRAMEWORKS

For Use By: Any organization seeking 3rd party validation of cybersecurity controls.

Scope/Area of Focus: Implementation of organization-wide security controls.

Audits: Formal examination performed annually by an accredited accounting firm under the American Institute of Certified Public Accountant (AICPA) system examination guidelines.

Many companies are required to demonstrate that their cybersecurity threats are managed effectively with controls and processes to identify, respond, mitigate, and recover from security incidents and breaches. The AICPA has created this cybersecurity risk management reporting framework to assist senior management, boards of directors, analysts, and stakeholders in gaining a better understanding of an organization's security efforts. The framework is a key component of the SOC for Cybersecurity evaluation, through which a CPA reports on an organization's enterprise-wide cybersecurity risk management program. SOC for Cybersecurity is useful for any organization whose clients and stakeholders would be affected by a cyber-attack, and is especially beneficial for B2B companies.

SOX

Full Name: Sarbanes-Oxley Act of 2002.

For Use By: Primarily used by publicly traded companies to validate the protection of financial data.

Scope/Area of Focus: Organization-wide controls that safeguard financial data.

Audits: To avoid conflicts of interests, companies hire independent auditors who are not involved in their other audits. The process will also help protect the company from insider threats. The SOX auditor will examine four internal security controls as part of an organization's yearly audit. These four controls are access, security, data backup, and change management. Understanding internal control weaknesses is key for organizations to establish adequate protection of their financial records.

SOX, short for the Sarbanes-Oxley Act of 2002, is required for all public companies. This includes banks, tech companies, and education. SOX stresses a number of areas, including the auditing of different aspects of the network, such as infrastructure, vulnerabilities, and other controls. It also encourages the automation of processes and managing risks. In particular, SOX looks at 5 base principle and believes that all systems should work to meet these requirements. These principles are Security, Availability, Processing Integrity, Confidentiality, and Privacy. Overall, while SOX is only required for public companies, it can be a good standard for all companies.

GDPR

Full Name: General Data Protection Regulation.

For Use By: Organizations handling personally identifiable information (PII) of the European Union (EU) citizens.

Scope/Area of Focus: Implementation of controls related to safeguarding and managing PII of EU citizens.

Audits: A formal independent audit is not required unless an organization is identified as not adhering to principles of GDPR, which may be discovered through customer complaints of violations.

The General Data Protection Regulation (GDPR) is a European legislation that was created to protect the data of all European Union (EU) citizens. Every company that works or deals with consumer data in the EU must comply with GDPR. GDPR compliance covers the following principles: Lawfulness, Fairness and Transparency, Purpose limitation, Data minimization, Accuracy, Storage limitation, Integrity and Confidentiality, and Accountability. In practice, a few examples of these principles include storing accurate and current data, only collecting the data that is needed, and properly disposing of data upon request ("Right to be forgotten").

FERPA

Full Name: Family Education Rights and Privacy Act.

For Use By: Educational institutions and organizations handling student PII and other student data.

Scope/Area of Focus: Implementation of security controls focused on student data.

Audits: FERPA is administered by the Family Policy Compliance Office (FPCO) in the Department of Education. In most educational institutions, the registrar's office, Legal Affairs or the Department of Academic Affairs of the organization are responsible for FERPA compliance and auditing.

FERPA is a federal law that protects the confidentiality, integrity, and availability of student educational records. The Act applies to any public or private, secondary, or post-secondary school that receives federal funds. The majority of public schools and virtually all private schools are covered by FERPA because they receive a degree of federal funding. FERPA is intended to spell out the rights of a student and the responsibilities of the educational institution. Students can file a FERPA violation with the Department of Education, which can result in civil litigation, or loss of funding and education grants for an institution.

FERPA is a standard that uses guidance from NIST SP 800-171, which provides an overview of how higher education can handle controlled unclassified information (CUI), like educational records. It also covers NIST SP 800-53, which touches on data protection and privacy obligations. NIST SP 800-53 addresses security from a functionality and assurance perspective meaning it goes beyond simply implementing a control to measuring the control's security capability. This is particularly important as a data breach resulting from a control failure can constitute a FERPA violation.

CCPA

Full Name: California Consumer Privacy Act.

For Use By: Organizations handling personally identifiable information (PII) of California citizens.

Scope/Area of Focus: Implementation of controls related to safeguarding and managing PII of California or citizens.

Audits: A formal independent audit is not required, unless an organization is identified as not adhering to principles of CCPA, which may be discovered through customer complaints of violations.

The California Consumer Privacy Act (CCPA) is a law pertaining to many companies working in California and/or collecting data from California residents. The goal of CCPA is to protect the California citizens from immoral personal data collection and improper use of personal data, while allowing the user to opt out of their data being sold. According to CCPA, the following must be provided to the user: The description of personal information disclosure must be provided, an option to opt out of selling their information must be available, and the company must obtain consent to sell their data.

OTHER STATE REQUIREMENTS

For Use By: Organizations handling personally identifiable information (PII) of citizens of specific states.

Scope/Area of Focus: Implementation of controls related to safeguarding and managing financial information and/or PII of citizens of specific states.

Audits: A formal independent audit is generally not required, unless an organization is identified as not adhering to the principles of the applicable requirements, which may be discovered through customer complaints.

Maine Act to Protect the Privacy of Online Consumer Information prevents Internet service providers (ISPs) from using customer personal information unless the customer express consent. ISPs must also take reasonable measures to protect customers' personal information. This information includes personally identifying information, but also information from Internet access services, like web history, geolocation data, device identifiers and other data points that could potentially identify individuals.

Massachusetts Bill H.4806190th (2017–2018) lays out actions that must be taken to protect consumers from a security breach. This includes disclosing the company of the entity breached, in addition to the person responsible for the breach. The breach notifications must also expose the type of personal information compromised and offer free credit monitoring services for at least 18 months to residents whose social security numbers have been affected by a breach.

Much like CCPA, Nevada Senate Bill 220 mandates that businesses should offer consumers opt-out options regarding the sales of their personal information. Website operators must post new information in their privacy policies, like the category of data collected and where data is being shared. Violation can result from a $5,000 penalty per instance, to a permanent injunction, if not fixed within 30 days.

New York State Department of Financial Services (DFS) 23 NYCRR 500 places certain minimum cybersecurity requirements on all financial institutions regulated under the DFS. A DFS entity is classified as having more than 10 employees, $5 million in yearly revenue, or assets exceeding $10 million. Any DFS-regulated organization conducting business in New York is required to establish an internal cyber program to protect their assets. Additionally, they must assess their risk profile and address the risks in a timely manner. NYCRR 500 also requires that they meet obligations, such as designating a Chief Information Security Officer, implement policies related to third-party data control and report data breaches, regardless of their size.

Unless the United States can agree on a national standard, new state regulations will continue to arise. It is important to research regulations in the states where most of your customers reside, especially if your organization holds Personally Identifiable Information (PII).

OPERATIONALIZATION OF COMPLIANCE

Compliance of varying flavors has become part of everyday cybersecurity life, be it a NIST or CMMC requirement for Defense contractors, Payment Card Industry (PCI), SOC from AICPA, ISO, NCUA and the list continues to grow. There are several inescapable truths for all compliance frameworks. They all overlap at some point, they sound overwhelming if you are not familiar with them, they add overhead to your KTLO and cybersecurity resources, and they can all create a 30 to 90-day fire drill while the auditor is onsite.

There is a way to simplify compliance, regardless of the type, and that is with the operationalization of the process. This will especially benefit you if you have multiple compliance framework requirements. We'll discuss the Operationalization of PCI Compliance, but the basic ideas can be applied to any compliance framework.

Compliance is here to stay. It used to only apply to select industries and organizations but new frameworks are being developed continuously and now the congress is debating federally mandated standards (God help us, 535 lawyers don't equal 1 cybersecurity expert). Get used to the idea that soon, everyone will have a compliance requirement to follow. Do it willingly now, or be forced into it later with a tighter timeline.

Operationalization of PCI as an Example

The Payment Card Industry Data Security Standard or simply "PCI," is an ever-growing compliance framework that has forced businesses of all sizes and industries to rethink how to not only apply the PCI controls effectively, but how to maintain a continuous state of compliance and keep up with the annual assessment. In the following pages, we will use PCI as the example requirement to describe the operationalization approach that leverages existing internal cross-functional teams to achieve any type of compliance.

By providing PCI training/recertification to your critical KTLO and security team members and implementing an operationalized PCI program that works with an external Qualified Security Assessor (QSA), the enterprise is able to maintain a self-contained PCI assessing process that becomes a year-round standard practice, not an annual 30 to 90-day fire drill. It also becomes clear that when companies invest in staff training, they have significant savings on consultant fees and time needed to be compliant.

Compliance Today

For many of us, PCI life today consists of uncalculated technical decisions based on a limited knowledge and understanding of the Payment Card Industry Data Security Standard and its reporting and compliance requirements. Most businesses that are involved with PCI and its Data Security Standard are struggling to understand and maintain scope, gather adequate security control supporting evidence, properly manage their QSA (yes, they can be managed; their word is not law and you can disagree with them—more on that later), and properly manage their acquiring banks. That will all be repeated again every year, with costs increasing as complexity to meet the compliance standard increases.

IT departments are struggling to keep up with continuous patching, scanning and evidence-gathering activities, including the configurations of tools that may be necessary to ensure their systems maintain compliance, let alone ensure that their KTLO needs are managed. Limited manpower and lack of proper project planning are also contributors to the consistent struggle felt by PCI participating organizations for the first 2–5 years.

A Better Approach

Unlike other compliance requirements, PCI makes it critical to ensure that you clearly define those systems and applications that are in scope and, if possible, utilize network segmentation to separate them from systems performing non-PCI functions. This will limit the infrastructure that will need to be documented and reviewed by the QSA. Some companies have taken the approach that the whole enterprise should be PCI compliant. However, there are problems with scaling and maintaining that compliance method. Most of the time, decisions like that are made by someone in management who doesn't understand the workload and the resources required for the full enterprise to become compliant.

Use your KTLO teams to operationalize tasks, like evidence gathering, documentation and process review, and other risk specific processes required annually for your organization's specific PCI reporting requirements, by using internal employees as well as contractors. A QSA can then be leveraged to provide the external validation of the internally operationalized processes and review the evidence library. This will ultimately reduce the cost of compliance and ensure proper utilization of IT resources.

Why Your Operations Team Is Important

Your KTLO team is important because PCI requires annual assessments, so an operational approach is necessary. The PCI Security Standards Council supplies the necessary tools and training for businesses to be self-sufficient at pcisecuritystandards.org. The best and most qualified people to carry out this work are the operations resources and your internal security team, who in their daily duties manage your organization's IT systems and applications.

> *"Compliance is a by-product of good cybersecurity. However, being compliant does not mean you are secure."*
> —Ancient Infosec Proverb

It is important to understand that anytime a 3rd Party QSA assesses your environment, they will have limited knowledge on the details that make up your systems, applications, and networks, compared to your internal staff. This limited knowledge can often lead to PCI "scope creep," which is manifested as unnecessary work or even purchases recommended by the QSA. This is why we have mentioned previously that you can disagree with the QSA. Quite often a QSA's lack of a complete understanding of your environment may lead them to recommend or require solutions that are not needed for your enterprise. Current and proper documentation of your process, standards, policies, applications and infrastructure is critical to having a high value return from a 3rd party QSA.

Reduce Costs by Investing in Your People

Currently, Mid-Quadrant Qualified Security Assessor (QSA) firms are charging on average $300-$450 per hour. The initial number of hours required for your audit will depend on the size of your organization and how well you have deployed and documented your technical footprint. The initial costs can be high but if the organization is able to mature its compliance program, these engagements can get less expensive year after year, until there is a maintenance plateau. IT and Compliance Managers should not forget that the PCI DSS changes every 3 years to comply with emerging threats and the assessment and reporting are required annually.

Investing in your employees is a good idea for multiple reasons and if you already have a plan to provide educational benefits, PCI training is a great addition. PCI Training will bring clarity and insight to the very people that will be required to do the work to ensure compliance, work like control implementation and evidence gathering of control states. It is critical to your success that your technical people understand the PCI requirements. This will strengthen your ability to maintain compliance and reduce any confusion that can exist inside the teams. Having a unified voice of understanding will bring confidence to the 3rd party QSA and allow your internal IT experts to gain PCI governance expertise. They will support the ongoing requirements and automate tasks, where possible. The investment in PCI training will save your organization a lot of money in the long term.

Auditors are not gods. You can disagree with them!

Engaging the Auditor

When the QSA first comes on site for the initial meeting, it is important to have your key technical and security resources in the meeting with your compliance team. While in small to mid-size companies the security team and the compliance team may be the same people, at larger companies these are usually different departments and not having all the critical resources present can lead to challenges with completing the audit quickly and accurately. PCI, by all accounts, is the most technical of the compliance requirements you will face because it deals with securing data and the enterprise as a whole. If defining the scope and providing direction for the PCI audit is managed by a non-technical compliance officer who does not fully grasp compensating controls, business justifications, and technical necessities, it can lead to not only a painful audit but a more expensive one that can add risk to the company. Ensure your technical teams are engaged from day one in order to mitigate scope creep and the potential pain of the audit.

IMPLEMENTING AN OPERATIONALIZED PCI PROGRAM

For our purposes we are using PCI as an example. We understand that all compliance frameworks have their own subtle variations of requirements and some don't need auditors. Regardless of your compliance requirements, the principles found through the next pages will serve you well in simplifying your compliance process, especially if you have multiple compliance requirements.

Why Operationalize?

As discussed in the overview, Operationalization of PCI compliance will save time, money, and make this a much less painful process in the long run when it can be managed by internal resources. Our intent is to provide an overview of the operationalization of compliance as well as to define requirements for quarterly, semi-annual, or annual evidence collection and document review. We will propose to perform semi-annual PCI self-audits conducted by the ISAs and PCI-Ps (PCI Professionals) on the security team, biannual penetration testing, perimeter scanning at minimum monthly, internal and external vulnerability remediation categorized as high monthly, semi-annual evidence PCI evidence gathering, centralized repository for documentation, policy, and procedure including a requirement for the annual document review and process updates. The goal of operationalizing PCI is to ensure the continued compliance with PCI, not to attain PCI compliance once annually. Implementing a continual process on an annual basis will limit the issues and uncertainty that have been experienced in previous audits. This framework will provide an efficient utilization of resources and reduce the strain on KTLO activities that occur during the annual audit.

> *"One who doesn't define the scope of a project will be quickly overwhelmed."*
> —Ancient Infosec Proverb

Scope

Compliance will impact any business unit, including human resources, sales, accounting, engineering, development and operations teams as well as any application that is subject to or supports PCI compliance. However, the most impacted resources will be the security and operations teams as they will be responsible for conducting most of the work, ensuring that PCI is properly operationalized, that compliance is maintained and resources utilized properly.

The Problem

As we have stated previously, compliance exercises in the first 2–5 years can be an extremely stressful time. It is filled with uncertainty about the scope of compliance as well as the new experience of having the internal organization subject to an external auditor. Unfortunately, PCI Compliance is not only a requirement to take credit cards, but it is often required by customers and vendors. With the ever-changing cybersecurity landscape, the sophistication of cyber criminals, and the invention of cybersecurity insurance, compliance and security will continue to evolve and become more complex. Some forms of compliance are becoming a mandatory requirement for doing business, regardless the size of the company. In short, a PCI or even a SOC 2 audit can be painful and chaotic without a plan. However, using an operationalized, documented, and centralized approach to PCI compliance will make for an efficient streamlined approach with little impact on standard KTLO functions and activities.

Recommendations

The following recommendations have been gained through years of experience with painful trial and error, pushing through compliance audits. The list is not exhaustive, we can always learn something new, but these recommendations are tried, true, and successful.

> *"Those who don't understand history are doomed to repeat it. Those who don't learn from the pain of their first audit are doomed to walk a very rough road."*
> —Ancient Infosec Proverb

Major Activities, With Little Cost!

1. Semi-annual self-assessment—Even though you may not be a QSA, any PCI-P on your staff can perform an assessment of your current PCI compliance state. Annual self-assessment will limit the surprises that will ultimately occur if you wait until the QSA and the external pen testers show up.

2. Semi-annual penetration testing — It never hurts to conduct your own pen tests, in between 3rd party tests, with internal qualified resources, if you have them.

3. Semi-annual internal and external PCI scans, either utilizing your own cloud based scanning tool or engaging a cybersecurity company to perform monthly scans and provide a report.

The Plan

1. Identify evidence to be gathered per requirement for PCI (*See Example Evidence Matrix at the end of this chapter*).

2. Establish a workflow process. Many teams use applications, like JIRA, Archer, MS Teams or even SharePoint.

3. Create and maintain a secure centralized storage repository for internal audit evidence storage.

4. Identify contacts on the operations team for evidence and ticket assignment. Work with the operations' team managers to ensure their support.

    a) Use several resources per team, if possible, in order to avoid single points of failure and to provide everyone the opportunity to gain some experience.

    b) It is critical to your success to have to buy-in from operations' management on the quarterly review. They need to be educated on how this, in the long run, will save them time and wear on their resources.

5. Automate evidence gathering where possible.

6. Focus evidence gathering on issues you have had in the past, like legacy hardware, applications or operating systems, so there are no surprises.

    a) Have a documented process in place for the decommission of legacy hardware, applications and software.

7. Gather and validate evidence on new compliance requirements for that calendar year.

8. Gather and validate the evidence as it relates to the current version of PCI-DSS.

9. Update documentation to reflect the current year.

    a) Have stakeholders review documentation and make updates that reflect changes in the organization since the last audit.

    b) Store all documentation that will be presented to auditors in a single secure and documented location.

10. Remediate any issues you discover.

11. Ensure that your vulnerability management process and documentation are up to date for each quarter.

12. Document all compensating controls.

13. Document and validate all business justifications every 90 days.

14. Document lessons learned after every audit and self-assessment.

15. Restart the monthly or quarterly requirements right after the last audit is done. With practice, it will simply become routine and part of your ongoing operations.

Documentation and Evidence Management

1. Create a centralized and secure evidence data storage for current and previous year's audits. We repeatedly hear, *"We have a different auditor this year so last year's evidence won't work."* This is simply not true. We also hear, *"What exactly do we need to provide to the auditor?"* You will accelerate evidence gathering by operationalizing compliance and providing your evidence-gathering teams with examples from previous years. While you may have a new auditor every year, the auditor is not setting the compliance standard. PCI-DSS is the arbiter of the standards with which you must comply. Last year's evidence, stored in a centralized repository, will enable you to provide your operational staff with examples of the evidence that you need to provide to the auditor.

    a. Quarterly or semi-annual evidence gathering is preferred to validate accuracy. A documented method of retrieval of evidence will also ensure the process is known and utilized.

    b. To round out this section, it is recommended to create a standard naming convention for evidence requirements such as "control_device-name_date" don't just create a data dump.

OPERATIONALIZATION OF COMPLIANCE

It's scary how many companies just drop their evidence collections in random locations and don't maintain their repositories. It's a simple concept: Store your data in a well-organized repository year over year to give yourself an example of what you needed for the last audit.

2. Annual documentation review—PCI, like any other compliance standard, requires that standardized documentation be maintained for processes, such as hiring and termination of employees, data storage and destruction, user provisioning, hardware security, etc. Work with your HR team to ensure these documents are complete. The goal of the company should be to standardize documentation across business units, whenever possible, and have this stored centrally. This may not impact small to medium-sized companies but it can have negative consequences on large companies during an audit. Visit ***http://resources.cyberrants.com*** for additional information.

3. Network, Data Flow, and Infrastructure Diagrams.

    a) Create a diagram standard, utilizing a tool like Microsoft Visio, and then document network and application connectivity to that standard.

    b) Require diagrams for all new application or network changes, prior to implementation and security signoff.

    c) Create a centralized repository for network, application, and data center diagrams.

4. Document your server, desktop, and application builds, including your hardening standards.

5. Wherever possible, utilize a centralized and standardized base of images for all systems and applications.

6. Ensure that build books are up to date.

7. Ensure that all firewall changes which impact compliance are documented with:

    a) Exact details of what was changed. It is not enough to simple mention that a firewall was updated. The ports and protocols also need to be documented.

    b) The justification for the change.

    c) The testing method and results.

    d) Temporary changes need to have a stated duration, including the implementation and revocation dates.

    e) Document new application or resource access requests

8. Update architectural documents, diagrams, and build books with every change that impacts a PCI application.

Vulnerability Management (All Year Long)

1. Scan! Internal and External.

2. Develop a VMP Plan with remediation to support findings.

3. Patching and vulnerability management should be a monthly activity.

4. Decommissioning EOL (end of life) devices—create and document a decommissioning process. If EOL devices cannot be replaced, have a documented plan to replace them as soon as possible. Also document the compensating controls or business justification in place to show your security posture and to demonstrate the need to keep the EOL devices in place.

OPERATIONALIZATION OF COMPLIANCE

Additional Recommendations

1. Do not assume that a vendor is securely storing your data. Audit them and establish a Third-Party Assessment (TPA) process if you don't have one.

2. Implement a centralized inventory management tool that is continuously updated.

3. Wherever possible, automate the compliance process. Not only the work flow but the actual evidence gathering.

4. Utilize CIS compliance for server builds and their environment.

5. Establishing a build standard and documenting the process will take the guesswork out of the hardening process.

Final Thoughts About Operationalization

Assessments and formal audits are required year after year as a part of the compliance process for many frameworks. So, as long as the organization chooses or is forced to align with specific requirements, audits will become part of standard operations. Governing organizations of compliance frameworks offer valuable support. For example, the PCI Security Standards Council offers PCI training and certification to empower participating organizations. Entrust your people and leverage the training offered by the council to offset the costs and the work required annually for audits and certifications.

Remember that compliance is not security. Compliance is a by-product of a hardened technology environment with educated and empowered employees, using standardized and repeatable processes. Setting the focus on effective cybersecurity, above compliance, eliminates the catch-up routine that can plague your organization and its employees.

EXAMPLE: EVIDENCE MATRIX FOR PCI V.3

Evidence Type	Evidence Required	PCI Req. Met by Evidence
Document	Roles and Responsibilities (Tool Team RACI Chart High Level).	1.1.5: 7x: 8x
Document	Network Diagram showing all required and installed (Tool) components, ports and protocols. Include description on diagram of port group & purpose.	1.1.6
ScreenShot	If applicable, a screenshot of the endpoint (Tool) agent reporting back to the console (from management station).	1.4
Document	Process to manage (Tool) (Admin guide).	1.5
Document	Hardening Guide for (Tool).	2.1: 2.2: 5.2b:6.1:6.2
ScreenShot	If applicable, a screenshot of the (Tool) providing monitoring for known, justified insecure services and current SSL/TLS versions in use (Screenshot).	2.2.3
ScreenShot	Screenshot of AD Security group for (Tool) restricted access (for Tool admins).	2.2.4: 7x: 8x
ScreenShot	Screenshot of method used for (Tool) admin to log in and preform duties (e.g. SSH/VPN/TLS/SSL).	2.3

DO YOU REALLY NEED ANOTHER CYBERSECURITY TOOL?

The proliferation and race to market newer, better, and stable security tools has thoroughly saturated the IT world. Who hasn't walked through a trade show and seen booth after both of the latest and greatest tools? Before implementing anything new for our clients, we always ask, *"Do you really need another tool?"* Tools are positioned as labor-saving applications that will provide the security that your enterprise requires. They allow you to run lean, with minimal staff or minimal contractors/consultants required to manage the enterprise (something the board, investors, and accounting team like). The problem is that unless you are a Fortune 100 company, running lean means you may only have one SME. That SME may have a partially trained backup with minimal experience because they have their own tool or set of tools and operational responsibilities. Then, one day, they both leave or a decision is made to cut staff and you lose key resources…now what?

Everyone gets excited by cool new tools to help save them from cyber criminals. People purchase based on a value-added reseller's (VAR's) recommendations and industry reviews but rarely think about deployment, configuration, tuning, management, backup management, architecture or depreciation of the technology. Maybe this is why most security tools we see are only configured to 40% maturity. In this state, that means getting 100% of the value out of the tool is impossible to achieve.

Silent Sector recommends taking a deep breath and stop buying tools, at least for a moment. We take a different point of view from the rest of the cybersecurity industry and make recommendations that are guaranteed to offend some. Read on. It will make sense in a minute.

First, a few questions about your organization:

1. Can you name all the security, monitoring, logging, prevention, provisioning, hardening, deployment and detection tools in your enterprise?
2. If you can, do you know who owns them?
3. Do you know who the SME that has the day-to-day responsibility for the tool?
4. If you can name the SME, ask them if they have the time they need every day, while performing regular duties, to digest and use all the data provided by the tool (outside of critical alerts and putting out fires). What is their answer?
5. Is the data provided by the tool actually useful to the organization?
6. How much did you spend on tools and maintenance last year?
7. Do you have a geographically dispersed security team?
8. Do you have a use case for every cybersecurity need that the organization is using a technology to meet?
9. Do you have a comparative analysis for the security tool requirements you need vs. the tools available and how their technology meets or exceeds your needs?

We are by no means proposing that you abandon the use of security tools. Silent Sector uses multiple tools for pen testing, compliance tracking, vulnerability scanning, and other activities as needed. We are also tool and technology agnostic. While we have our preferences, we do not sell software, tools, or hardware. Instead we strive to make clients successful with what they already have, encouraging that they only buy new tools if they really are needed for a strong security posture.

Many clients have purchased more tools through the years than they can begin to use, some of which have overlapping capability. Worse yet, many tools were sitting dormant, while getting renewed annually, because the subject matter expert (SME) that knew the tool has moved on (we all know IT people move around from job to job for numerous reasons and that is a topic for another time). Eventually, the SME's backup also moves on, then the other backup, and the manager that originally approved the tool. Meanwhile, the company keeps renewing the license of the tool that no one uses. They also keep acquiring the next new tool that will "solve all the problems." It is a perpetual cycle of throwing money out the window.

Of course, you are asking, *"Wait are you really that jaded? Do you just need a hug? Are you really Comic Book Guy from the Simpsons?"* We have had long careers in IT and security at all levels with all types of companies imaginable, consulted a long time, and seen things that would leave most speechless. Because of this, we left corporate IT to start our own company. Between the three choices above, we'd go with jaded (hugs are nice too) but we are hopeful that we can help open eyes and change this wasteful cycle.

Let us share an example. Described below are two companies different in scope and volume, yet their circumstances are eerily familiar.

- Company A is a medium-sized regional company with about 1,500 employees. With compliance requirements they were late in understanding their needs for IT security. They have cycled through multiple senior level IT management teams, including C-level and directors. As a result, they had to rebuild their IT staff multiple times and as such, lost most, if not all, of the tribal knowledge in IT.

- Company B is a large international company with 7,500 employees. They grew rapidly through acquisition but as a result, lost not only tribal knowledge and key SMEs but the mid-level management that handled the acquisition, as well as most (if not all) of the senior IT leadership. This included complete security teams as well as entire IT staffs, other than those that possessed the IP that justified the purchase of the company.

The circumstances are similar for both companies. As new teams of IT management and resources took control of each environment, they have each brought experiences with tools and solutions that they have used at previous roles in their careers. They have each made their own cases and as a result, tool sets and solutions were purchased. Due to business requirements, change in management direction, or simple turnover, these tool sets and solutions went untended or not fully deployed. Replacements were hired who may have had knowledge of the existing tool sets but had a tool set or management style they preferred, so a case was made to purchase new tools. Then at some point due to business requirements, change in management direction, or simple turnover these tools and solutions went untended or not fully deployed. Replacements were hired who may have had knowledge of the current tool set but had a new tool set and management style they preferred, so a case was made to purchase new tools. Then at some point due to business requirements, change in management direction, or simple turnover, these tools and solutions went untended or not fully deployed…. Are we repeating ourselves?

If the situation above sounds familiar, don't worry; there is a way out of this cycle. Warning: It might be a little painful so strap on your chain mail.

YOU REALLY NEED ANOTHER CYBERSECURITY TOOL?

> *"Doing the right thing is like organizing CAT 5 cable. Regardless of how painful it may be today, tomorrow will be that much more pleasant."*
>
> —Ancient Infosec Proverb

1. **STOP!** Don't buy anything new until you have completed an inventory of every tool in your enterprise.

2. Identify the cost of every tool you own as well as their maintenance and support fees.

3. Identify what each tool does, if they are utilized to their full capacity, or at the very least, what the modules you own will do.

4. Identify the SMEs responsible for each tool (if one of the identified SME is that guy that used to sit in the cubicle by Janice, it might be a bad sign if you haven't seen him, or Janice for that matter, in a while).

5. Identify where the tools you own overlap.

6. Identify any gaps that you need to address which are not covered by your existing tools.

7. Determine what tools are still needed and those that you can decommission. Be sure to let your purchasing department know not to renew those licenses. You will save not only on the tools but also on the infrastructure costs.

8. Put together a team and a project plan to fully deploy the tools you have decided to keep.

9. Determine if you have the in-house expertise to deploy the tools to their full capacity. If not, engage professional services from tool providers or experienced implementors.

10. Make company sponsored training on the tools a priority for your SMEs. Quite often, the tool companies provide it for free or for minimal cost.

11. One challenge in larger organizations is that tool management may be dispersed in different geographic locations and across multiple teams. To simplify management, Silent Sector recommends that clients identify a single geographic location and team to consolidate tool management. This will also make cross-training easier.

12. Complete requirements gathering and purchase additional modules needed or bring in additional resources to complete the deployment of existing tools.

13. Create a centralized inventory of tools and document repository.

14. Get to work deploying, configuring, and leveraging the tools you have decided to keep.

15. Decommission tools no longer required and their infrastructure.

16. Document (we know, everyone in IT hates this) but document everything you have done, every setting, service account, every piece of infrastructure, port, protocol, and connection, with justification for what you did. The idea being that if your SME gets hit by a bus on the way to work or wins the lottery and walks away, someone can pick up where they left off.

17. Diagram the tool—create a Visio diagram with a graphic representation of what you have documented. This is a little more fun than documentation (but only a little).

18. Use your tools and delegate a SME with two backup persons.

19. Utilize job swapping for cross-training opportunities. This will help backups learn in a live environment, while the primary SME is still engaged (and not just waiting out their two-week notice).

20. Have your boss give you and your team a bonus for saving the company money and being so brave and innovative! In all seriousness, attaching a bonus, as a percentage of money saved, to your team would go a long way for motivation.

> *"One who appreciates their team is appreciated by their team."*
> —Ancient Infosec Proverb

REACTIVE DEFENSE VS. PROACTIVE CYBERSECURITY

WHY CAN'T WE HACK BACK AGAINST CYBERCRIMINALS? WHY CAN'T WE FIGHT BACK?

We've all heard the saying, *"The strongest defense is a good offense."* Unfortunately, in the world of cybersecurity, with the exception of law enforcement, the bad guys are the only ones who get to play offense. Black Hat versus White Hat is not as bad as the Harlem Globetrotters vs the Washington Generals, but sometimes, after reading all these news reports about breaches and hacks, it certainly feels like it.

No one wants to be a punching bag. This is why we often get asked, *"Why can't we fight back against cybercriminals? Don't we have the skills? Are they better than us?"* Long story short, the White Hats (good guys) have the same bullets in their guns as the Black Hats (bad guys). Black Hats have two things going for them that White Hats don't, unless they are dedicated threat hunters. The Black Hats have time to plan and research an attack, plus the anonymity that the Internet provides.

Hacking back against cyber criminals is currently illegal for non-law enforcement personnel but fear not, Congress has introduced two bills (as of this writing) to address the issue of hacking back. Who better than 535 non-technical "lawyers" to determine the best way for technologists to fight back against cyber criminals? Makes perfect sense, right?

This is not a left or right issue, nor red or blue, so please don't make the mistake of considering this a political rant. We're talking about a bill that has broad bipartisan support. Rather, this is just our own jaded opinion about non-technologists wading into technical issues without proper information.

The original Active Cyber Defense Certainty Act (H.R. 4036), or ACDC for short, was introduced to the house by Representative Tom Graves (R-GA 14th District) on October 12, 2017. The bill was reintroduced in June of 2019 with bipartisan support and became H.R. 3270. The intent of the bill, as stated in the bill's summary states:

"To amend title 18, United States Code, to provide a defense to prosecution for fraud and related activity in connection with computers for persons defending against unauthorized intrusions into their computers, and for other purposes."

The intent of the bill is to protect from prosecution companies that react proactively to a cyberattack on their enterprise. That being said, the hurdles and red tape the bill requires would make counterattack nearly impossible due to the flexibility in hacker infrastructure, including the use of bot farms, virtual machines (VMs), and the anonymity that the Internet provides. It also includes the requirement for getting a plan approved by the FBI in order to counterattack. By the way, the FBI isn't a fan of the bill to begin with.

Long story short, this bill is a bad idea. We know... We would love to be able to zap a hacker, just like you probably would, but in reality, it is simply not feasible. There is a better way and that is through the use of proactive cybersecurity defense, some of which is actually acknowledged in the bill. We have included parts of this bill here to illustrate why this is a bad idea. However, please go ahead and do a search on the bill, if you're curious, and review it for yourself.

The following protocols are recommended by proponents of the bill for fighting back:

1. Establish attribution of the attack.
2. Disrupt the cyberattack without damaging another party's computers or other property.
3. Retrieve and destroy stolen or compromised files.

4. Monitor the behavior of an attacker.

5. Utilize beaconing technology.

Lawyers and politicians, as well intentioned as they may be, are NOT cybersecurity experts!

Key Congressional Findings Stated:

(1) Cyber fraud and related cyber-enabled crimes pose a severe threat to the national security and economic vitality of the United States.

(2) As a result of the unique nature of cybercrime, it is very difficult for law enforcement to respond to and prosecute cybercrime in a timely manner, leading to the existing low level of deterrence and a rapidly growing threat. In 2017, the Department of Justice prosecuted only 165 cases of computer fraud. Congress determines that this status quo is unacceptable and that if left unchecked, the trend in cybercrime will only continue to deteriorate.

(3) Cybercriminals have developed new tactics for monetizing the proceeds of their criminal acts, making it likely that the criminal activity will be further incentivized in the absence of reforms to current law allowing for new cyber tools and deterrence methods for defenders.

(4) When a citizen or United States business is victimized as the result of such crime, the first recourse should be to report the crime to law enforcement and seek to improve defensive measures.

(5) Congress also acknowledges that many cyberattacks could be prevented through improved cyber defensive practices, including

enhanced training, strong passwords, and routine updating and patching to computer systems.

(6) Congress determines that the use of active cyber defense techniques, when properly applied, can also assist in improving defenses and deterring cybercrime.

(7) Congress also acknowledges that many private entities are increasingly concerned with stemming the growth of dark web-based cyber-enabled crimes. The Department of Justice should attempt to clarify the proper protocol for entities who are engaged in active cyber defense in the dark web so that these defenders can return private property such as intellectual property and financial records gathered inadvertently.

(8) Congress also recognizes that while federal agencies will need to prioritize cyber incidents of national significance, there is the potential to assist the private sector by being more responsive to reports of crime through different reporting mechanisms. Many cybercrimes are not responded to in a timely manner, thus creating significant uncertainty for many businesses and individuals.

(9) Computer defenders should also exercise extreme caution to avoid violating the law of any other nation where an attacker's computer may reside.

(10) Congress holds that active cyber defense techniques should only be used by qualified defenders with a high degree of confidence in attribution, and that extreme caution should be taken to avoid impacting intermediary computers or resulting in an escalating cycle of cyber activity.

(11) It is the purpose of this Act to provide legal certainty by clarifying the type of tools and techniques that defenders can use that exceed the boundaries of their own computer network.

REACTIVE DEFENSE VS. PROACTIVE CYBERSECURITY

Some of the above, like Number 1, are pretty obvious. Okay, well, all of them are, but this is your Congress ladies and gentlemen. At least they are trying to act. The findings above can be broken down in the following categories:

- Obvious to any cybersecurity professional: Numbers 1–4.

- Congress acknowledging there are other options: Numbers 4–6 (last sentence of 4) would be proactive cybersecurity and defense, which all companies should be doing.

- What government should be doing: Numbers 7–8—The government needs more resources to fight this type of crime. The issue with this is really two-fold, first the shortage of trained and qualified cybersecurity professionals and second, the disparity in pay between government employees and the private sector.

- Defining what an active defender can do: Numbers 9–11 define unrealistic requirements for reacting to a cyberattack for the following reasons:

    - Number 9: Computer/Cyber laws are not standardized globally, which is why so many cybercrimes go unpunished. You can get yourself in a whole lot of trouble with another country if you hack back.

    - Number 10: Who or what defines a qualified defender? Is it everyone with a Certified Ethical Hacker (CEH) credential? It could be a truly scary scenario to turn an army of script kiddies loose as a cyber posse!

    - Number 10: How do you prevent damage and fight back? The damage is already done when a vulnerability is exploited on a computer.

    - Number 11: The government will define the tools? There is so much in that statement and way of thinking to give us pause and fill us with concern.

The unintended consequences and collateral damage of mal-attribution, misconfiguration, or hitting a botnet or zombie computer, should give anyone a moment of pause in supporting this bill. The chances of unintended damage to the innocent are too great.

Exception for the Use of Attributional Technology

We are going to chop out most of this section but the key piece, which tells us why this is just a bad idea:

> *"(B) the program, code, or command does not result in the destruction of data or result in an impairment of the essential operating functionality of the attacker's computer system, or intentionally create a backdoor enabling intrusive access into the attacker's computer system."*

The above statement is the technology equivalent of sending an army to war with instructions to only shoot the enemy in the leg or arm... Just wound them.

Sec. 4. Exclusion from Prosecution for Certain Computer Crimes for Those Taking Active Cyber Defense Measures.

Section 1030 of title 18, United States Code, is amended by adding at the end the following:

> *"(l) Active Cyber Defense Measures Not A Violation. —"*

> *"(1) GENERALLY. —It is a defense to a criminal prosecution under this section that the conduct constituting the offense was an active cyber defense measure."*

> *"(2) INAPPLICABILITY TO CIVIL ACTION.—The defense against prosecution created by this section does not prevent a United States person or entity who is targeted by an active defense measure from seeking a civil remedy, including compensatory damages or injunctive relief pursuant to subsection (g)."*

Section 4 above calls out acts that a "defender" can perform and escape persecution; however, they can still be sued if they do any damage to a U.S. Citizen's computer. We have one question regarding point number 1, what is going to stop an attacker from claiming that all they were really doing was "an active defense measure"? This would, in essence, eliminate criminal prosecution and limit them to civil liability.

Sec. 5. Notification Requirement for The Use of Active Cyber Defense Measures.

Section 1030 of title 18, United States Code, is amended by adding the following:

"(m) Notification Requirement For The Use Of Active Cyber Defense Measures."

"(1) GENERALLY. —A defender who uses an active cyber defense measure under the preceding section must notify the FBI National Cyber Investigative Joint Task Force and receive a response from the FBI acknowledging receipt of the notification prior to using the measure."

"(2) REQUIRED INFORMATION.—Notification must include the type of cyber breach that the person or entity was a victim of, the intended target of the active cyber defense measure, the steps the defender plans to take to preserve evidence of the attacker's criminal cyber intrusion, as well as the steps they plan to prevent damage to intermediary computers not under the ownership of the attacker and other information requested by the FBI to assist with oversight."

We'll give you a minute to stop rolling your eyes and shaking your head. The FBI doesn't like this bill for a myriad of reasons, including the fact that it might interfere with an active investigation or the tracking of a cybercriminal. Per Christopher Wray, head of the FBI at the time of this writing, *"We don't think it is a good idea for private industry to take it upon themselves to retaliate by hacking back at somebody who hacked them."* If the bill passes and you are required to get FBI approval, knowing how they feel, do you think you will get FBI approval in time to actually track the attacker, find their infrastructure before they mask their IPs, tear down their VMs, or release their bots?

Sec. 6. Voluntary Preemptive Review of Active Cyber Defense Measures.

We took out sections (a) and (c). Section (a) calls for a pilot program that lasts two years and (c) allows the FBI to prioritize the requests that come to them for approval, which would be based on availability of resources.

> *(b) Advance Review.—A defender who intends to prepare an active defense measure under section 4 may submit their notification to the FBI National Cyber Investigative Joint Task Force in advance of its use so that the FBI and other agencies can review the notification and provide its assessment on how the proposed active defense measure may be amended to better conform to federal law, the terms of section 4, and improve the technical operation of the measure.*

Have you ever waited in line at the DMV? In essence, with a pilot program that lasts two years and the requirement of a formal review of the plan, including the technology that will be used, this will be outdated before they can put into action. What are you doing to protect your data in the interim? Buck up, we have an answer for you. It was in the earlier chapter called, "Proactive Cybersecurity" so you already know the good stuff!

WHERE DO MSPS FIT IN A CYBERSECURITY PROGRAM?

Managed Service Providers (MSPs) can be a tremendous asset to an organization, often fulfilling needs that cannot or should not be handled internally. IT departments leverage MSPs for specific purposes, allowing organizations to outsource functions and freeing up internal resources to focus on critical business initiatives. We see many organizations working harmoniously together with their MSPs, benefiting from the increase in capabilities, while reducing costs.

For smaller companies that cannot support internal IT staff, it often makes sense to engage an MSP to manage all IT operations. A good MSP can design and implement a plan that scales with the growth of an emerging company, ramping up services as the budget allows.

With the emergence of cybersecurity as a hot topic and a critical requirement, many IT providers and MSPs are pushing to gain a piece of the market. The increasing demand for cybersecurity and the complexity of the subject causes many organizations to seek a "one stop technology provider" in an attempt to offload the burden. As a result, it has become common for IT providers and MSPs to add cybersecurity to their suite of IT solutions. Doing so allows them to gain new clients and prevents the loss of current clients.

However, cybersecurity and IT are complementary business components but very different disciplines. Combining the two and treating them as one set of services often results in negative consequences for clients. Cybersecurity and IT require different skill sets, ways of thinking, and experienced practitioners in their respective fields.

CYBER RANTS

This is why mature, and larger, proactive organizations have a cybersecurity department that is managed separately from their IT department. The two disciplines, teams, and resources are independent but support each other's efforts. This approach creates a checks and balances effect, benefiting the organization as a whole. The IT team keeps operations running and scales as the business grows. The cybersecurity team covers the risk management operations, and participates in change management, risk assessments, governance, and compliance, while providing cybersecurity guidance to the IT team as needed.

The biggest problem with the managed IT services industry selling cybersecurity is that the services are often represented as a complete solution, promising protection for their clients. Unsuspecting and untrained decision makers are led to place their trust in solutions that often fall short of providing adequate defense against cyber-attacks. This is not mere opinion. We are witnessing a rising number of breaches caused by industry-wide problems, some of which will be discussed through this chapter.

We often hear, *"quality is more important than quantity,"* and in recent years threat actors have adopted this viewpoint. Instead of pursuing a large number of victims, which may or may not reap rewards, cybercriminals can be more successful in targeting the MSPs who commonly administer the IT infrastructure for businesses. In essence, the reliance on the MSP for cyber protection becomes a single point of failure for many organizations. This increase of MSP focused attacks is signaling a need to evaluate current MSP security competence.

Having the IT team or 3rd party IT companies responsible for cybersecurity makes about as much sense as having the bookkeeper audit their own books.

WHERE DO MSPS FIT IN A CYBERSECURITY PROGRAM?

Again, a MSP relationship is highly valuable for many organizations. Our purpose here is to shed light on a topic that is misunderstood and misrepresented in the IT industry. You'll begin to understand where a MSP fits in a security program and where it does not. We will also demonstrate why it is a conflict of interest, creating significant risk, to place the responsibility of your security program on the same people handling the ongoing IT operations.

What is a MSP?

A managed service provider (MSP) often identifies itself as an IT company or IT provider. It is simply a company that handles all or a portion of its clients' IT requirements, using an assortment of technologies designed by others. MSPs serve a wide range of clientele but primarily focus on small and mid-size organizations.

Many MSPs function as the IT equivalent of a "one-stop-shop." From implementation to management and upgrades, they offer a wide spectrum of services. This is an appealing option for many organizations because sustaining day-to-day IT operations can be a tiresome, yet necessary task, that impedes many small and emerging companies from ever reaching their business objectives or increasing their revenue.

It is estimated that most businesses currently spend at least 80 percent of their in-house IT budget and resources on KTLO activities, simply maintaining their existing IT infrastructure and applications. This is where the chief appeal for MSPs comes in. They seek to alleviate burdens of internal IT resources for an organization so it can focus on core objectives. They are not only capable of setting up their IT infrastructure, but they can also handle the monitoring and reporting on services.

The list of services that MSPs commonly offer include network management, help desk support, cloud and data management, as well as backup tasks. Additionally, as the name implies, MSPs can manage tasks, like file organization, printing administration, and even communication technologies, such as VoIP. Nowadays, these services are critical to the success of any business wanting to keep up with opportunities driven by technology and market trends. Additionally, technological advancements can be used to bring in clients who are seeking innovative and unique vendors instead of an organization that simply mimics their competitors. This is why staying ahead of trends is essential for businesses that want to seek competitive advantages and forecast better economic prospects.

Good IT leadership is in very high demand and sometimes hard to obtain for many organizations. This can cause problems while communicating or aligning their enterprise support model. It will also affect ongoing projects with their purpose, impact, and objectives. As a result, the current projects handled by the IT department may not fully align to meet the business plan and growth model of the enterprise.

In response to this, numerous security organizations have published models to help companies avoid unwarranted IT spending. For example, ISACA has certifications, such as Certified in Risk and Information Systems Control (CRISC), which aims to guide professionals managing IT risk, including IT projects, for an organization. CRISC dictates that all IT should be looked at in the order of strategic goals, business units, and finally the information systems (IS) level. The strategic goals are the big picture or the overarching purpose for the organization's existence. The business units are the departments working to fulfill the mission's objectives while the IS level is the equipment that affects the unit's ability to operate.

Internal IT departments, dealing with limited resources, can find their time consumed with KTLO operations and urgent requests. As a result, they are seldom informed of security risk models or have time to implement them. It is not unusual for IT departments to exercise unmaintainable business cases, like the routine break/fix method. Like treading water this method is not cohesive nor justifiable to obtain funds as it only maintains the business in a status quo rather than expanding capabilities and meeting objectives. In those situations, the in-house IT

WHERE DO MSPS FIT IN A CYBERSECURITY PROGRAM?

department usually proposes budgets and every line item is scrutinized. Items are frequently dismissed by the executive leadership, due to the lack of IT strategy and alignment with business objectives. New IT projects require business cases to illustrate whether the initiative will help the organization make or save money. If it does not address at least one of these requirements, what contribution does the initiative offer?

Good MSPs execute cohesive and well-conceived plans which validate the outsourcing of IT for many organizations. They have leverage over the in-house IT model by itself because they can offer infrastructure scalability and flexibility at lower cost. This means an organization using an MSP can allocate IT capital as needed, which usually results in cost savings. These reduced costs can alleviate funds for new IT capabilities or initiatives.

Additionally, most MSPs can operate within multiple types of IT infrastructures, regardless if they are cloud, on-premise or hybrid. This creates a motivation to improve technologies over time. On the other hand, an internal IT department with poor leadership can end up living by a "if it's not broke, don't fix it" mindset, which leads to avoiding attempts to fix or improve infrastructure that is seemingly sufficient.

MSPs are emerging everywhere as the reliance on IT infrastructure increases and businesses start to witness how technology can be utilized as a competitive advantage.

MSPs are quickly scaling and expanding their portfolios as demand is increasing. Alas, the MSP dilemma begins. In order to take advantage of new clientele, MSPs have also positioned themselves as well-rounded security companies due to the shortage of cybersecurity resources and the increasing costs. Recent statistics show that 85% of all U.S. companies do not have the security resources that they need, either in-house or on retainer. This frightening reality is why many organizations are starting to consult their MSPs to handle their cybersecurity needs. When in fact, much of what is required for a proactive cybersecurity program is exceedingly outside of the capabilities of the vast majority of MSPs.

MSPs often handle specific functions that play important roles in a cybersecurity program but rarely provide complete and adequate cybersecurity protection, not to mention the alignment with compliance requirements and the conflicts of interest that result from such an arrangement.

CISA Notification About MSPs

The concerns about MSPs marketing themselves security experts only became an issue recently. Early in 2019, Rex Booth, the Chief of Cyber Threat Analysis for the Cyber Security and Infrastructure Security Agency (CISA), shared that an ongoing campaign of cyberattacks had been specifically targeting MSPs. This has been transpiring since 2014, when CISA first started observing an increase in MSP attacks, however, at the end of 2018 they witnessed a severe surge. This prompted CISA, an organization whose mission is to "protect the Internet," to publicly disclose their findings.

The Department of Homeland Security (DHS) has since linked the string of MSP attacks to the Chinese government. More specifically, they have identified an Advanced Persistent Threat (APT) known as APT 10, which they have been monitoring for years. DHS has determined that APT10 is sponsored by the Ministry of State Security in China, which is allegedly providing them with major financial backing.

When an adversary is categorized as an APT, it means they are very powerful and highly motivated. They pose a severe threat because they are not and cannot just be anyone off the street. While the media and pop culture have indoctrinated most people with the idea that hackers are just hooded individuals in a basement, the reality is quite different. APTs, however, are not this archetype nor mindless automation. They are rather sophisticated groups that use strategic principles to gain information and unauthorized access to information systems. What sets APTs apart from other threat actors is their objectives. Their goal is to maintain long-term access to a target and not necessarily execute a specific task. In order to do this, they often rely on advanced abilities. They use stealth methods to evade detection and maintain long-term IS access. What makes APTs particularly dangerous to defend against? Should they choose to infiltrate an organization, they will most likely succeed, because they have both the resources and determination.

Can MSPs Mitigate the Risk and Provide Proper Security?

MSPs can offer some level of security, but realistically, the degree might be questionable. Unfortunately, the barriers they face to become security-oriented are tall. For one, their mindset must shift from modeling infrastructure with a strict IT approach to now include security. This entails recognizing how adversaries might try to circumvent controls placed on information systems (IS). Controls, which often impede small businesses, need to be agile. Taking, for example, something as primitive as access control, which is used to authenticate, authorize, and allow account IS usage. It could also be manipulated to gain unauthorized IS access and cover an adversary's footsteps. As luck would have it, when MSP personnel implements access control with a security mindset, they can deter and prevent vector exploitation from commonly used IT platforms.

Migrating from solely using uptime as a measure of success is another hurdle MSPs must overcome. Instead, they should use a combination of security measurements like compliance with industry standards, patched vulnerabilities, and click-through rates. Additionally, MSPs must leave behind the habit of selling products that they are either not experienced in supporting or which are not required for their clients. However, even though it is very appealing to sell cheaper obsolete products with identical descriptions as emerging products, it is not worth taking the additional responsibility.

This can be evaluated in a way that takes into account the rapid advancement of technology. Consider how floppy disks used to be the de facto storage system, but now are rarely seen. Removable media, such as tapes and optical drives, are not only significantly slower to use but also downright inefficient when compared to modern solutions. With the transition to online storage, most new computers now lack a floppy or DVD drive slot and we are even starting to see the deprecation of USB ports.

The path for MSPs to properly break into security necessitates that they refrain from making security product sales the core of their business model. Without the proper expertise to design and implement a wholistic cybersecurity program, the products being promoted are often not aligned with framework requirements and do little to actually mitigate risk. Any poorly run MSPs claiming *"We have always done it this way,"* are in no condition to offer security services because the threat landscape is evolving at an incomprehensible rate that mandates relentless research. It is a fair assumption to say that most MSPs are not necessarily aware of their shortcomings, but no one can argue that it is irresponsible and unethical to sell cybersecurity in a way that implies complete protection.

However, investing time into the research of IT solutions and security defenses will reap long-term benefits for MSPs and some are more proactive than others. This means spending capital, personnel and time to soak up the required security knowledge is necessary if MSPs want to offer security services. Practical starting areas will range from researching vendor products, to asking industry security experts what they use and recommend. It also involves changing the MSPs' business and operational structure to reduce conflicts of interest.

Issues of MSPs Acting as Security Companies

Traditionally, security was viewed as the final step after deployment. However, with standard IT functioning as the mainstay of many businesses today, IT work is now married to cybersecurity. This means security must be considered at every step of the infrastructure design through the deployment phase. Furthermore, when organizations contemplate integrating products with the cloud or adopting new applications, security should be one of the first things that come to mind. Moreover, to truly be effective, organizations must also integrate security with their end users. After all, these are the individuals who interact the most with IT and IS. Users could be system developers, server admins, vendors or any other personnel who come into contact with the system or will come into contact at some point. Integrating security objectives with IT infrastructure can be confusing and tedious. This is why it comes as no surprise that businesses are attracted to the idea of outsourcing this to MSPs.

Additionally, due to the evolving portfolio of what MSPs offer, the resulting security needs that need to be met are seemingly infinite. This has led to MSPs offering services, such as security hardening and defense, that are out of their scope and beyond the capabilities of their resources. In fact, many end up outsourcing this work and white-labeling the reports so it appears as if the work was done in-house.

An MSP does not become a cybersecurity company just because they "have a guy" who got a security certification. Yes, this does happen and far too often. You'd be amazed at the number of companies that provide general IT or an unrelated technical service one day and are "cybersecurity" companies the next.

MSP Attacks to Infiltrate the U.S., a National Security Issue?

From a rather ingenious angle, APT10 has been leveraging the use of MSPs as an entry point to forward the Chinese political agenda, such as the "5-year plan." This is a series of blueprints for social and economic developments in China, which includes aspects like achieving a "moderately prosperous society" and "innovation-driven development." CISA confirmed that the targeting of MSP-like organizations indicates the advancement of Chinese objectives. Experts also believe that the recent cyberattacks linked to China have underlying motives to steal trade secrets, commit espionage, and make technological advancements.

On average, it takes an organization two hundred and six days to detect a breach. Consider for a second that APT10 breached 100 United States MSPs. This would contribute to utter chaos in the economic and social world. Small to medium-sized businesses are vital to the health of the U.S. economy, the backbone if you will. They not only create the majority of jobs but also advance the Gross Domestic Product and innovation in Middle-class America. Small to medium-sized businesses commonly employ individuals seeking to invent new products or solutions while dodging the corporate politics commonly associated with larger enterprises. Moreover, these businesses help prevent viable monopolies while also fostering ingenuity among employees.

Compromising an MSP enables threat actors to reach their economic development goals while also impairing U.S. establishments since many corporations rely on smaller organizations to outsource critical business functions and manufacturing. They could also leverage stolen intellectual property and profit off it. Whether premeditated or not, targeting MSPs is expanding the possibility to stunt the U.S. economy from the inside out. As MSPs become more aware that they are at a higher risk for specialized attacks, they can now enlist in better prevention and detection techniques.

MSP Security Mindfulness and Complacency with Current Defense Strategies

The issue is not that MSPs are unaware that their clients are putting a high level of trust in their security abilities. Rather, the issue revolves around them not being prepared to handle the security of an IT system from initiation to deprecation. For example, when an MSP is deploying a customer relationship management (CRM) or payroll application, they are assuming that the software is protected because it is proprietary. They might also have a sense of complacency towards the security of a system because they have used it for several years.

Additionally, MSPs might feel that clients are getting what they view as "adequate defenses," so there is no need to do anything new.

However, with the threat landscape changing at an unprecedented rate and adversaries perfecting their attack methods, MSPs must pick up new defense strategies. For example, consider a firewall—something so simple, yet critical to the securing of a network. Despite sounding the same on paper, firewall offerings are not the same. Hence, putting in a solution that is 80% effective, when compared to a better alternative, still puts a 20% gap in the defense component. Without wholistic planning and highly trained cybersecurity practitioners, MSPs will not have a grasp of the necessary compensating controls required to protect older systems that an organization may require to operate. This results in a security gap, straight out of the gate, as a consequence of the poor product choice.

Managing firewalls and other security-related infrastructure is a very important task but they don't constitute a proactive cybersecurity program and effective risk management.

Furthermore, since MSPs are not security centric, it can be very enticing to accept vendor contracts that include "free firewall hardware when you buy a 2-year license." The profit margins on such offers are also seemingly beneficial for both the MSP and the vendor. As a consequence, MSPs are misguided if they believe that it is a good idea to offer products they have little to no understanding of, in order to save a few bucks or underbid the competition.

Options for Small Businesses with Very Limited Resources

Unfortunately, small businesses struggle tremendously with cybersecurity. Their shortage of budget often prohibits them from engaging specialized cybersecurity firms. Usually, their shortage of adequate time and knowledge also prohibits the do-it-yourself approach. *So, what can a small business do to protect themselves?*

Fortunately, businesses in this category have much smaller and less sophisticated infrastructure when compared to mid-market and large organizations. In this case, the business's IT provider or MSP is the most realistic solution until the organization grows to the point where dedicated cybersecurity support is needed.

In this section, we'll cover considerations for MSPs and IT providers serving small businesses. If you lead a small business, consider this information as you discuss security with the people managing your IT.

When working with smaller clients, it is important for MSPs to accept that budgeting issues can quickly arise. However, to avoid damaging their reputation, MSPs should still adhere to a standardized security package covering the basics. This package could be waived by the client signing an acknowledgment, but it should be presented as being critical. Of course, there could be variations offered, such as endpoint protection, backups, email security, etc. but the key is making it a non-negotiable part of the deal.

Smaller clients might still push back by advocating that they are not at risk since they do not have a lot of assets or anything valuable to steal. Emphasizing that no one is exempt from an attack can overcome this uninformed thinking. They should also be reminded about the severe legal and industry fines for not applying a basic level of security. Walking away from a client who is not open to security will undoubtedly be difficult. However, MSPs must recognize that declining to sign on a client for the monthly recurring revenue might be a preferable option than risking the customer being breached, thus creating a legal and reputational issue for all parties involved.

Unfortunately, many lifestyle and health-related organizations, like medical clinics who often hold PII/PHI/PCI data, seldom have hefty security budgets. For this reason, MSPs must often wager those philosophical issues, like requiring clients who cannot afford the standard security package to sign a waiver and segment their IS from other clients or even walk away.

MSPs offering security solutions should make every attempt to convey to their clients the importance of appropriate funding for securing their IT infrastructure. The art of persuasion entails presenting evidence that action is needed and then offering a solution that solves the problem. In which case, translating technical jargon into high-level business terms is one technique MSPs can utilize. From their perspective, a business proposal needs to be crisp and authoritative. In this case, it means that the MSP should demonstrate their grasp on the job to be done and enough details to exhibit their expertise without including unnecessary technical specifications. This could be achieved by focusing on the unintended problems that weak security creates and with an emphasis on how implementing technologies can help shrink these complications.

For example, illustrating the need to purchase an expensive Unified Threat Management Platform (UTM) would be difficult if it is presented as being useful for its next-generation firewall capabilities, extensive switching, and deep packet inspection features. By communicating, instead, that the need to purchase a UTM is to keep systems free from infection, which will support the mission goal of minimal work outages and save on hours for the help desk—there is a higher level of success. They can still offer more details later, as needed for the technical specifications.

When clients start to apprehend the importance of fund allocation for security during the IT infrastructure planning phase, they may realize that their budget does not leave a lot of room for the products recommended by the MSP. In these circumstances, MSPs might recommend phasing in security. The idea is that rather than sell mediocre products that predispose organizations to gaps, they can do a gradual upgrade as the organization grows. These upgrades also apply to compensating controls for the needed hardware. Typically, a client's priority starts with endpoint security. This might be met by adding anti-virus and encryption to a workstation.

However, as an organization's infrastructure advances, so must the controls to protect hardware against threats. Thus, budgeting for compensating controls starts to surface as the hardware evolves.

Consider the endpoint with effective anti-virus and encryption. While the chances of malware taking over are slim, it is still a possibility. In this case, an MSP can later offer compensating controls such as business email security or even an endpoint solution that does micro-segmentation or sandboxing of an infected device. This will keep the client from overextending their budget, while still leading them to a path of security. Moreover, mastering security product selection and overcoming stiff funding restrictions come from on the field experience. In the context of security, we're often told, *"something is better than nothing,"* and unfortunately, many MSPs opt for lower priced and hence lower quality solutions that set organizations up for serious security cavities that can be later exploited.

Misguided Metrics

When an MSP offers products and designs for IT infrastructure, they use features and uptime as a measure of quality, rather than security. Failure to pick a product that has had proper code analysis will predispose clients to exploitable vulnerabilities. Furthermore, when selecting products, MSPs, and sadly some customers, use the price tag as a metric of quality. Looking at what threat or vulnerabilities each new service could introduce to a business's existing infrastructure is a concept known as threat modeling. The willingness to bring in new products without threat modeling presents issues that can enable malicious activity, compromise data, and even result in a loss of service.

Additionally, bringing in new products is not always necessary. For one, MSP personnel commonly do not understand asset identification and risk management. This can lead to overspending on security defenses for assets that are not business critical. Not all assets need the same level of protection, as they are not vulnerable to the same vectors. The misconception that deploying a security defense is equivalent to eliminating a threat or risk is one that diminishes with security experience.

Vocabulary Gaps

Despite security vocabulary being monotonous and often overly complicated, it is critical to the success of security professionals and organizations seeking to offer security services. MSPs often use security buzzwords, like "ransomware" and "APTs," without truly understanding their significance. The inability to recite what a threat or vulnerability is leads to the inability to explain the purpose of certain services. Therein, from a management standpoint, that ambiguity makes the services not worth investing in.

Most MSPs understand that risk is exposure to some type of danger. MSP employees who lack prior security experience might wager that by implementing managerial, technical, and operational controls, one could eliminate all risk. Yet, veteran security professionals will know that risks can never be 100% eliminated. Some risks must be accepted and planned for. Furthermore, the hardware, software, and applications in IT will quickly go out-of-date. Meaning the IS controls implemented this week, to mitigate last month's threats, might be completely irrelevant next year.

Security Tools Gap Scan and Pen Test Difference

In cybersecurity, there is no "one tool fits all." The most effective way to protect a business against threats is layering different tools, security tests, and strategies. Businesses seeking security testing from MSPs must be aware that software and hardware tools are critical, but the most important tool is knowledge.

Think about something like the difference between a vulnerability scan and a penetration (pen) test. Vulnerability scans seek to proactively identify current and future threats on the network, such as cybercriminals, malware or improperly configured applications. While penetration tests actively try to exploit the discovered holes, demonstrating the outcomes from specific points of entry. Any MSP can kick off a network scan to detect vulnerabilities and give the report to the client without any logic or understanding behind the real threat or risk level. Pen testing has been simplified with the proliferation of Internet resources. However, the value from these security tests is considerably low when conducted by generic MSPs. This is by no intention of the MSP, but merely a result of trying to fill a need using intricate tools to identify gaps without the appropriate security practitioners to interpret the results.

To highlight this discrepancy, reflect on a newly hired grocery store manager. In the first few weeks, they are unaware why inventory and sales are not adding up; however, with time they start to observe a particular thief. Pretty soon they are identifying all noticeable vectors this thief, or thieves take and counteracting them. Going forward, this manager can apply these anti-theft practices to other stores and prevent threat actors from taking advantage of flaws. Anti-theft practices resemble various pen test types, such as web application, client side, wireless, physical and social engineering. Network pen tests are the most common and in-demand because they involve finding network infrastructure vulnerabilities. However, solely relying on a network pen test to secure an organization is like the store manager putting a luxury item on the top shelf to prevent theft.

In order to glean the most information, it is strongly recommended that organizations seek pen tests and network scans from dedicated cybersecurity services companies. IT generalists lack experience, yet promote their security tests as "industry standard," are assuming that their methods are enough to fortify client's defense. In reality, adversaries will tailor their methods to each target and use a vast number of tools, payloads, and methodologies to exploit weaknesses. Some companies are a lot like new managers, they mean well, but are confined to their limited experience, predispositions, and security knowledge.

Security Formula Gaps

Keeping in mind that budget dictates most business decisions, security experts commonly use formulas to quantify which controls or products are worth investing time and capital. Most MSPs do not have the same capabilities to apply security formulas or calculations to quantify spending as qualified security professionals. Dedicated security practitioners are apt to make rational spending decisions and commonly have formalized this understanding by attaining advanced certifications, like the CRISC. They can use their knowledge to validate the effectiveness and financial feasibility of a security control to evaluate the true cost of implementing security controls. Determining the cost of employing a specific protection cannot be calculated until a risk assessment, vulnerability assessment, and control selection have been completed. If a safeguard value exceeds an asset's value, it is up to the client to decide whether the control is needed.

The knowledge to apply formulas and then communicate the security findings to clients takes experience and proficiency that is only held by experienced security professionals. It is one thing to simply punch numbers in, but it is another to articulate how these numbers affect security implementation and thus attain the highest level of security necessary for each asset.

Security Focused Learning

Information is changing at a rate faster than anyone can keep up with. For those not fully focused on cybersecurity, it is nearly impossible to stay up to date with security specific information. The failure of not understanding the implications of a new adversary or vulnerability can be devastating. Additionally, not staying up to date with information can result in recycling superfluous security services. Although reading headlines can generate a sense of "breach fatigue," it can help businesses avoid mistakes that other organizations have made. Professionals focused on operational IT and KTLO activities have a huge amount of responsibility and multiple initiatives demanding their focus at all times. It's a complex and unforgiving job. For that reason, it is simply unrealistic to expect both adequate IT operations and adequate security operations from the same resources.

> *"He who chases two rabbits catches none, as he who chases too many technical disciplines achieves expertise in none."*
> —Ancient InfoSec Proverb

Checking a Box to Be Compliant Rather Than Actually Being Secure

"Convenience over security," is a phrase echoed in the security industry to illustrate how taking the path of least resistance usually results in poor security outcomes. Becoming complacent with standards often comes at the cost of secure systems. This is particularly rampant in sectors like healthcare where organizations are already understaffed. Using an MSP to "check the box" for industry, regulatory and legal compliance is a major driver why organizations are seeking their support. To stay in operation, health-related organizations, like hospitals, are also required to adhere to standards set forth by HIPAA, which has created dilemmas in choosing between security and legal compliance. Many organizations feel at a crossroads, where remaining in operation is the priority and thus they opt for MSPs who can offer the path to compliance. This is why most MSPs are ramping up on compliance solutions rather than offering solid security options. Remember, being compliant is not equivalent to being secure.

Organizational Growth

It is no secret that technology drives modern business, but it is equally, if not more important, to focus on the security posture of a company for growth. Organizations require customer trust to grow, and frankly, there have been serious lacks on that front. Headlines are exposing new breaches and businesses must quickly address their mitigation efforts. While these efforts might serve to reassure some customers about the security of their data, they are not entirely convincing. Where were the proactive security measures? The ramifications after a breach extends beyond monetary loss for the organization, to also include customer relationship issues and damage to their reputation. This is why security must be factored in when considering organizational growth. The security that sufficed for 20 employees will not cut it when an organization reaches 200 employees. What does this have to do with MSPs?

Selecting an MSP is as much of an investment into a business as it is into customer trust. Capitalizing on customer trust only arises from proper information security, which is ultimately required for sustainable growth. Arguably, the growth of an organization is in the hands of their MSP's ability to secure their infrastructure, especially if they do not augment the MSP's efforts with dedicated cybersecurity expertise.

Why do APTs Target MSPs?

MSPs use remote management software to operate their client's IT infrastructure, giving them a "backdoor" in. This backdoor is intended to be used for legitimate purposes, such as installing updates and troubleshooting. It is important to highlight that the actual attacks to MSPs are possible due to the nature of backdoors. Furthermore, vulnerable business processes, such as insecure backdoors, are the most common weaknesses exploited by threat actors. This is why industry experts understand that when dealing with vulnerable processes it is pertinent to "layer security." Extra security measures, like utilizing long passphrases, password fail lockouts, multi-factor authentication, access control, air-gapped networks, etc. are not always common knowledge to MSP personnel. Unfortunately, this often becomes known after the fact, when they get breached and clients are affected.

Targeting MSPs is appealing because they are a gateway into many sectors and business types, providing incredible leverage for cyber criminals. Infiltrating a single MSP can create tunnels into the healthcare, education, and government industries; making them more than worthwhile. Adversaries, like APT10, have uncovered and started to take advantage of the force multiplier effect associated with breaching MSPs. In business, the Return on Investment (ROI) is used to calculate if something is worth doing. This same thinking applies to cybersecurity criminals. Rather than putting a significant amount of resources into a single entity's system, why not go after the operator who has access to many systems, especially if you know they are not equipped to defend against advanced cyberattacks?

From the perspective of a cybercriminal, MSPs are also an initiation point to launch other attacks and spread malicious software, such as ransomware. The direct management backdoor access that MSPs have into their clients' networks allows for an easy setup of ransomware campaigns. In recent years, threat actors have noticed and leveraged this pathway to distribute such malicious software to hundreds of different organizations at once by exploiting vulnerabilities in the remote management software. In addition, a compromise in an MSP's network could be used to pivot into their clients' networks. To make matters more intense, attacking MSPs has the highest chance of profit. APTs, like APT10, have recognized that through attacking MSPs they can infiltrate dozens of businesses with a single attack. This in itself is introducing a new risk of large-scale infection. Furthermore, targeting MSPs is low risk and high reward. Cybercrime rarely gets punished or even ascertained and even then, the hypothetical financial gain is more than enough to counter the risk of being discovered.

Real World Instance:

In July 2019, employees at Arbor Dental in Longview, Washington, noticed they could no longer view X-rays. They also noticed that their workstations and X-ray servers were glitching. Arbor Dental was just one of the dozens of dental practices in Oregon and Washington infected by a ransomware attack that prevented them from accessing patients' records, ultimately disrupting their business. What is noteworthy about this incident is that Arbor was not the intended target. Meaning, they were not staked out or on a list of "organizations to breach." Instead, they were infiltrated through PM Consultants Inc., their MSP. This provider was handling all firewalls, data backups, and software updates for those dentists.

Naturally, when Arbor realized that something was out of the ordinary, they immediately called their MSP. In the first week, calls to PM Consultants went straight to voicemail. It is only in the second week that an email was sent to clients to inform them that they had been breached.

The email stated:

"Due to the size and scale of the attack, we are not optimistic about the chances for a full or timely recovery... at this time we must recommend you seek outside technical assistance with the recovery of your data."

In the third week, PM Consultants notified their clients that they were shutting down the business. Shortly after, their phone and website were disconnected. At the time of writing this article, no new developments on PM Consultants have surfaced.

It is by no wrongdoing of the MSPs that they are being targeted. However, major implications arise when they position themselves as security companies to increase clientele. Despite several MSPs offering reliable security services, data storage, and support, others are ill-equipped and uninformed. They might have the mechanisms to protect against script kiddies and other less nefarious threats, but most basic practices are hopeless against threats like APT10. This simply drives home an important point: avoiding and effectively responding to modern attacks requires that MSPs provide employees with proper cybersecurity education and resources before offering services outside of their areas of focus.

What Can Organizations Relying on MSPs Do?

MSPs can greatly help business growth if there is a compatible match and if the relationship is handled properly. However, it is important to understand that outsourcing IT is not synonymous with handing over the reins and being pardoned of responsibility, as risk and duty cannot be entirely transferred. It is always the responsibility of the organization to verify that their MSP has proper security credentials and experience that can stand up to scrutiny in the event of a data breach.

Organizations must understand that choosing a dependable provider is a long-term investment. Undertaking the vital research and asking the right questions will protect this investment. The goal is to allow the business to not only flourish but do so in a secure manner that will grant them a competitive advantage, in a world where staying ahead of assailants is increasingly challenging.

Moreover, in organizations where security is not negotiable, it is completely acceptable to engage with a dedicated security company to assess the MSP and identify how they stack up against their claims to security. Consider the example of selecting a doctor. Patients do not go to a doctor who claims to have the best treatments, but the doctor who has been vouched for by other medical professionals as being competent in what they do. The same theory can be applied to MSP selection. Trust that they know what they're doing but verify by asking long-standing security companies for feedback. This will give some peace of mind to organizations requiring a certain level of security. It will also help to identify risks when working with less "security-oriented" MSPs.

Final Thoughts

MSPs are vital to many companies, especially small and mid-size, as they can increase productivity and reduce stress. However, it is becoming common for MSPs to overplay their cybersecurity capabilities so organizations should exercise extreme caution when relying on one to cover their security matters.

MSPs are usually well versed in the latest IT trends but often lack the knowledge to make critical security decisions. In order to meet the demands from a wide range of clients, MSPs are often diversifying their services and positioning themselves as security specialists. Yet, in reality, they are not adept nor putting in the effort to become knowledgeable on advanced security concepts or expert-approved products. As a result, we can expect adversaries to increase targeted attacks on MSPs because their lack of experience makes them low risk and high-profit victims.

While MSPs serve a vital role in the IT operations of many organizations, always remember that cybersecurity requires appropriate expertise, a defense in depth approach, and a series of checks and balances. Keep in mind that MSPs can perform specific security tasks but know that they don't replace a holistic and proactive cybersecurity program.

All of this boils down to the fact that each organization must maintain responsibility for its own security. Keep a series of checks and balances, eliminate conflicts of interest, and get the best support you can for the job. Leveraging dedicated cybersecurity professionals to work alongside your operational IT professionals is a requirement for an adequate cybersecurity program, despite the misleading sales messaging that runs rampant in the industry.

FINISHING THE RANT

Like any other specialized function, cybersecurity requires the right tools, processes, and people. Attorneys are hired to handle specific matters, insurance covers certain exposure, and engineers bring distinct skillsets. Cybersecurity is now a standard business requirement. Like all other aspects of business, it must be handled appropriately by dedicated professionals.

We hope that you now have a good understanding of what is involved in building a proactive cybersecurity program. You should be equipped to make better decisions in protecting your organization's clients, intellectual capital, revenue, reputation, and longevity. We believe that this knowledge will serve you well wherever you go in your career.

Remember, nobody goes at it alone and succeeds. Proactive cybersecurity starts with a leadership decision and commitment. It requires a team of people who bring different knowledge, experiences and resources to the table. It takes planning and process development, testing and assessment, continuous review and improvement. A solid understanding of what is real and what is hype in the cybersecurity industry is critical; remembering that there is no such thing as a one-size-fits-all approach. It will also bring the realization that people are more important than tools and that cybersecurity is an asset to organizations that make it one.

The fact that you were reading this guide shows that you are already taking the right steps. Regardless of how you feel about your organization's current security posture, know that appropriate protection is attainable and you can affect change. With the proper support, proactive cybersecurity is quicker and simpler than you might realize.

> *"One who knows about cybersecurity but takes no action is still vulnerable and soon finds ruin."*
> —Ancient Infosec Proverb

Building an effective cybersecurity posture is simply the right thing to do for your organization, staff, clients, and your own career. We encourage you to boldly take the next steps.

Find the cybersecurity firm and professionals best suited to serve your organization. Develop an understanding of your current risks and vulnerabilities. Finally, define and follow a plan to continuously improve security. Blend this plan with your ongoing operations and it will no longer seem like a monumental task.

The Silent Sector team is building and improving proactive cybersecurity programs for United States-based companies. Reach out to us if you'd like to discuss your needs, get answers to any questions you have, and find out if we are a fit to help your organization. However, you decide to move forward, we wish you absolute success in all your endeavors.

Rant complete… For now.

www.CyberRants.com | book@cyberrants.com

ABOUT SILENT SECTOR

SiLENTSECTOR
EXPERTISE-DRIVEN CYBERSECURITY

Until just a few years ago, we were busy protecting major organizations such as Wells Fargo, AAA and NASA from the inside. But we recognized that mid-market and emerging companies had limited access to cybersecurity resources and expertise, dangerously exposing them to cyberattacks. We created Silent Sector to address this threat by offering the expertise and customization of our enterprise experience to the mid-market and emerging organizations that need it most.

We're not just here to make a buck—we're here to make a difference. Mid-market and emerging companies are the heart and soul of the United States economy. Unfortunately, they are also the favorite target of cyber criminals because they are most vulnerable. Too often, budget limitations have forced mid-market organizations to settle for limited software instead of comprehensive, customized solution. But tools and software aren't the answer to cybersecurity, human expertise is.

Through our proprietary Expertise Impact Methodology™, we reduce costs with effective strategy, focusing on maximizing the value of the resources you already have. This gives you the power to attain solutions fully customized to your priorities, and the peace of mind to focus on profitability and growth.

The Silent Sector team provides the expertise and resources to transform your data and technologies into hard targets, so cybercriminals move on. While our team has worked extensively with large corporations, we now primarily serve organizations with 50–

5,000 employees in the healthcare, financial services, technology services, and manufacturing industries.

Silent Sector is an elite team of experienced and credentialed, U.S.-based cybersecurity professionals. We have served a wide variety of organizations across many industries. Each team member is hand-picked, credentialed, and vetted, forming a tight-knit group of experts that become an extension of your team.

Whether you're looking to tackle a specific project or need a continuous cybersecurity solution, we provide the services customized to your needs. Our team integrates with your in-house or outsourced technology professionals for seamless collaboration and development of a highly effective security posture.

We are not a "magic solution" or software platform. We are truly the boots on the ground, fighting to protect your organization from cyberattacks.

Contact Silent Sector

480-447-9658 | info@silentsector.com | www.silentsector.com

Locations in Phoenix, Arizona & Boise, Idaho—Serving clients nationwide, remotely and with on-site visits.

ABOUT THE AUTHORS

MICHAEL ROTONDO, Silent Sector

Partner—Head of Compliance & Cybersecurity Operations

Michael Rotondo has been engaged in all areas of IT during his career, which spans more than 25 years. He began with selling computer parts in the infancy of the IT industry, during the pre-dot.com era, in the early 1990s. He quickly transitioned to the operations and consulting side of the industry. Mike began his work in the compliance side of Cybersecurity in 2006, as part of the growing Archive and Compliance practice focused on Sarbanes Oxley. He has been on the bleeding edge of technology in the Cybersecurity Industry for almost 10 years, holding every position in IT from help desk to architect.

Michael's Technical Certifications and Affiliations:

CISSP	Certified Information Systems Security Professional
CRISC	Certified in Risk and Information Systems Control
CEH	Certified Ethical Hacker
CPT	Certified Penetration Tester
PCI-P	Payment Card Industry Professional

Member of ISC2, ISACA, and ISSA

LAURO CHAVEZ, Silent Sector

Partner—Head of Cybersecurity Strategy & Research

By age 10, Lauro was experimenting with BASIC on an old Atari and by age 15 he was managing his own Windows NT domain at home. He joined the U.S. Army, where he obtained more technical training in signal communications, cryptography, computer/network engineering, and automation. During this advanced training, it was discovered that Lauro had an aptitude for identifying security flaws through stress testing applications and systems. He provided system/network engineering and cybersecurity support to U.S. Army communications networks and for sensitive missions during Operation Enduring Freedom, in Afghanistan. After eight years of active duty and an honorable discharge, Lauro began working for the Department of Defense. He supported "black" projects, such as the Joint Strike Fighter, and other highly sensitive endeavors being developed by the U.S. Air Force and NASA.

Lauro went on to build his own cybersecurity consulting practice, helping more than 40 organizations develop cybersecurity programs, maintain a strong security posture, and meet compliance initiatives such as PCI, COBIT, FIPS-140, and NIST. His twenty-plus years of experience spans the system/network engineering, architecture, and GRC spaces. He is a founding partner of Silent Sector and a passionate advocate for privacy.

Lauro's Technical Certifications and Affiliations:

CRISC   Certified in Risk and Information Systems Control
Oracle Certified Expert   Oracle Solaris 10 Security Administrator
CCNP+S   Cisco Certified Network Professional +Security
PCI-P   Payment Card Industry Professional
OSCP   Offensive Security Certified Professional

ABOUT THE AUTHORS

ZACH FULLER, Silent Sector

Partner—Head of Business Operations & Strategy

Zach Fuller has built businesses in industries, including website design, information marketing, ecommerce, real estate investment, private equity, and cybersecurity. He served as a Green Beret in the U.S. Army, conducting highly sensitive combat operations in Afghanistan. Zach was awarded a Bronze Star Medal, Meritorious Service Medal, and other decorations for his actions overseas. He later went into real estate investment and private equity, building an investor relations team for the firm Caliber, where he held the role of Executive Vice President. He led his team to raise over $300,000,000 in private capital, making Caliber an Inc. 500 Fastest Growing Private Company in America. Zach is a founding partner of Silent Sector, where he is focused on changing the dynamic of the industry by showing the benefits and impact that security brings to proactive organizations.

Zach's Technical Certifications and Affiliations:

John F. Kennedy Special Warfare School Graduate
Certified Ethical Hacker
Certified Cyber Intelligence Professional
CompTIA Security+
CompTIA Network+
CompTIA A+

COMMON CYBERSECURITY TERMS TO KNOW

The following list contains many common cybersecurity terms to support your conversations about the topic. This is certainly not an exhaustive list. Consult Google for additional terms.

Access Controls: Any method permitting user access to specific data or technologies.

Access Management: Policies, procedures, and controls used to determine who can access information and how it is accessed.

Administrative Controls: Policies, procedures, and standards governing the actions of people and information systems.

Adware: means used to track individual Internet users and profile their behavior in order to display advertisements.

Annual Loss Expectancy (ALE): The yearly estimate of loss of an asset (ALE = ARO x SLE).

Annualized Rate of Occurrence (ARO): The probability that a loss will occur within the course of a year.

Attack Surface: Components of a system that may be compromised by an attacker.

Authentication: The process of providing a user's identity to a system using two or more pieces of information in order to gain access (i.e. username and password).

Bot: In the context of cybersecurity, it is malicious software that allows an attacker to control someone else's computer for malicious purposes. (Other types of bots are now used for communications, support or IoT.)

Botnet: Collection of software robots ("bots") running through the centralized control or an attacker.

Business Continuity Plan: A plan determining the business response to a disaster in order to keep core operations functioning.

Business Impact Analysis (BIA): The process of identifying the impact on a business, resulting from the interruption of a specific system.

Cookie: A file used to store identifying information on a web client system, usually for a browser.

Data Classification: Categorizing documents and data by the level of sensitivity, in order to assure proper handling and safekeeping.

Defense in Depth: Implementing several layers of protection in order to protect assets in the event of the failure of one or more layers.

Denial of Service (DOS) Attack: An attack against a computer or network that is designed to incapacitate the target.

Disaster Recovery Plan: A defined method of assessing, salvaging, repairing, and restoring damaged assets and facilities.

Gateway: A device on a network that translates various types of network traffic.

Hacktivist: A malicious individual who attacks systems for political or ideology motives.

Hardening: The process of making a system more resistant to attack.

Least Privilege: A principle that states that a person should only have access to systems and information required to perform their official duties.

Malware: Malicious code intended to disrupt or control a system.

Patch Management: The process of testing and installing patches to update systems.

COMMON CYBERSECURITY TERMS TO KNOW

Penetration Testing: A process used to identify and exploit vulnerabilities on a target system or application in order to understand and improve security.

Phishing: Fraudulent email messages attempting to lure a recipient into providing private information, such as login credentials.

Pretexting: A method of deception intended to collect sensitive information from an unknowing individual.

Risk Assessment: The process of examining a business or technology system to identify potential risks.

Rootkit: Malicious code designed to hide itself and avoid detection by anti-virus and other defensive measures.

Script Kiddie: A person with low level hacking skills who relies solely on tools built by others to break into systems.

Separation of Duties: A process where high-risk tasks require two or more individuals to carry out, with the intent of reducing the risk of fraud and other malicious activities.

Single Loss Expectancy (SLE): The cost of a single loss in the event of a particular breach or damage to a system (SLE = asset value x exposure factor).

Social Engineering: An attack where a malicious individual attempts to gain sensitive information from staff members, typically for gaining unauthorized access to protected systems.

Spear Phishing: A targeted email attack meant to mimic normal communications between individuals in order to entice the victim to perform a specific action for the attacker.

Spoofing: An attack where the assailant changes or mimics the origin of a message in an attempt to disrupt or control a system.

Spyware: Software that is used to collect Internet usage information from an individual's computer, usually malicious.

Virtual Private Network (VPN): An encrypted communication channel used to secure traffic between two networks.

Vulnerability: A weakness in a system that may open the system to risk.

Whaling: A phishing attack designed to specifically target executives or other high-profile individuals.

Zero-Day Exploit: A new malware that evades detection because it has not yet been widely recognized.

ADDITIONAL MATERIALS & RESOURCES

Access your Additional Materials & Resources referenced throughout this book at
http://resources.cyberrants.com

Made in the USA
Columbia, SC
30 April 2021